HAL LEONARD COUNTRY DECADE SERIES

THE 1950s

50 Great Songs from Country's Greatest Stars

ISBN 978-1-4234-0618-1

7777 W. BLUEMOUND RD. P.O.BOX 13819 MILWAUKEE, WI 53213

Visit Hal Leonard Online at
www.halleonard.com

CONTENTS

ALONE WITH YOU

Words and Music by FARON YOUNG,
LESTER VANADORE and ROY DRUSKY

A♭
4fr
E♭
3fr
A♭
4fr
How I'd love to be a - lone with you.
D♭
A♭
4fr
Just to be with you one night, you and me a - lone.
D♭
A♭
4fr
E♭
3fr
Kiss your lips and hold you tight and have you for my own.
A♭
4fr
D♭
This would be a joy un - end - ing, could be a real be - gin - ning.
Won't you try to be my ba - by, just for once and then, well, may - be

A♭
E♭
A♭
1
How I'd love to be a - lone with you.
I could al - ways be a - lone with you.
2
D♭
Well, won't you try to be my ba - by, just for once and then, well, may - be
A♭
E♭
A♭
I could al - ways be a - lone with you.
Then I could al - ways
E♭
A♭
be a - lone with you.

ALWAYS LATE WITH YOUR KISSES

Words and Music by BLACKIE CRAWFORD
and LEFTY FRIZZELL

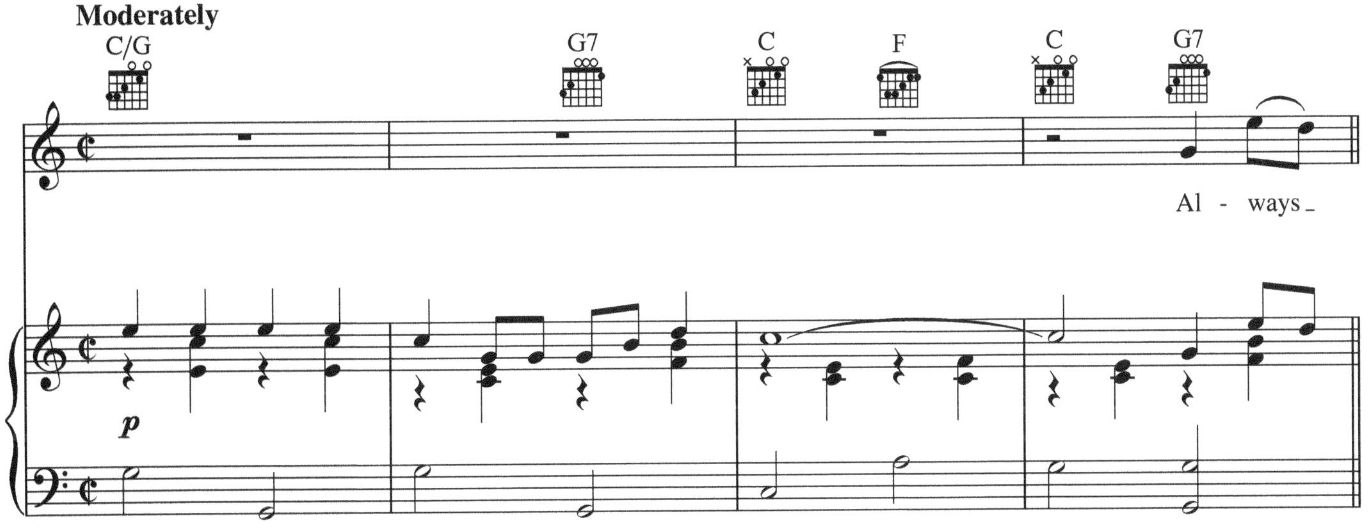

G7
C
stay?
Al - ways
late
F
C
with your kiss - es.
G7
C
Why, oh, why do you want to do me this way?
C7
F
C
How long do you think I can wait,

D7
G7
when you know you're al - ways late?
Al - ways
C
F
C
late
with your kiss - es.
G7
Why, oh, why do you want to do me this
C
F
1
C
G7
2
C
way?
Al - ways

BALLAD OF A TEENAGE QUEEN

Words and Music by
JACK CLEMENT

Additional Lyrics

4. Very soon she was a star, pretty house and shiny cars,
   Swimming pool and a fence around, but she missed her old home town.
   (But she missed her old home town.)
   All the world was at her door,
   All except the boy next door who worked at the candy store.
   Dream on, dream on, teenage queen, saddest girl we've ever seen.

5. Then one day the teenage star sold her house and all her cars.
   Gave up all her wealth and fame, left it all and caught a train.
   (Left it all and caught a train.)
   Do I have to tell you more?
   She came back to the boy next door who worked at the candy store.
   Now this story has some more. You'll hear it at the candy store.

THE BALLAD OF DAVY CROCKETT

from Walt Disney's DAVY CROCKETT

Words by TOM BLACKBURN
Music by GEORGE BRUNS

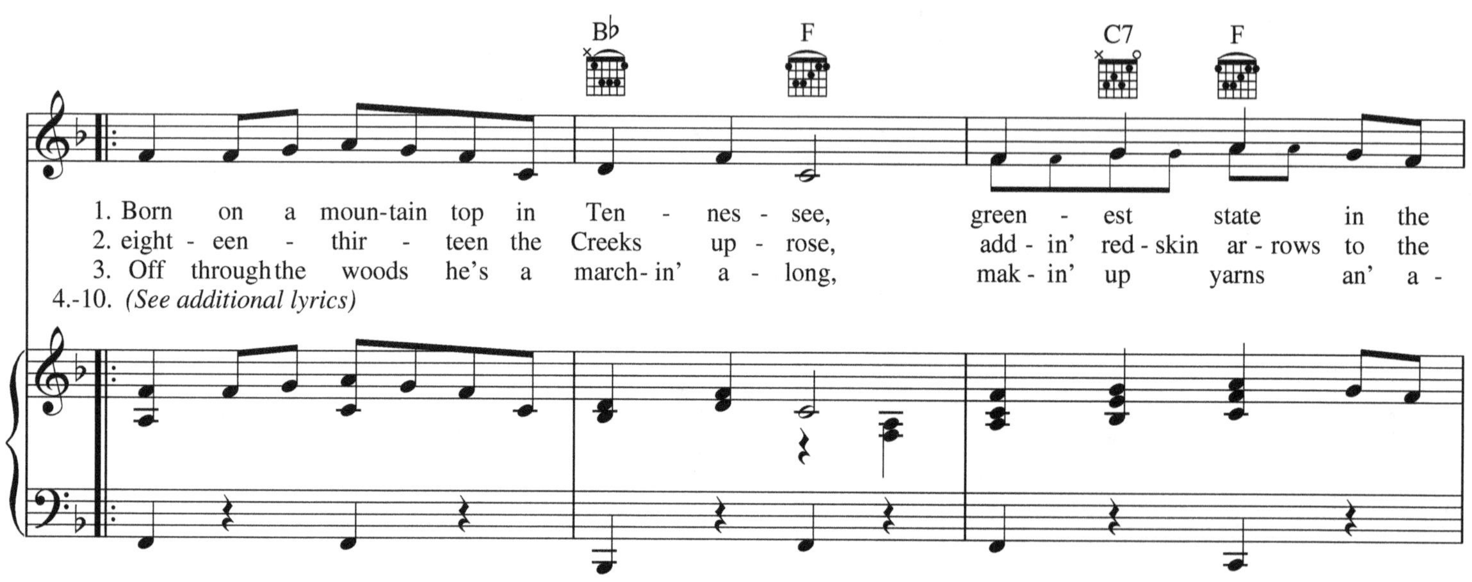

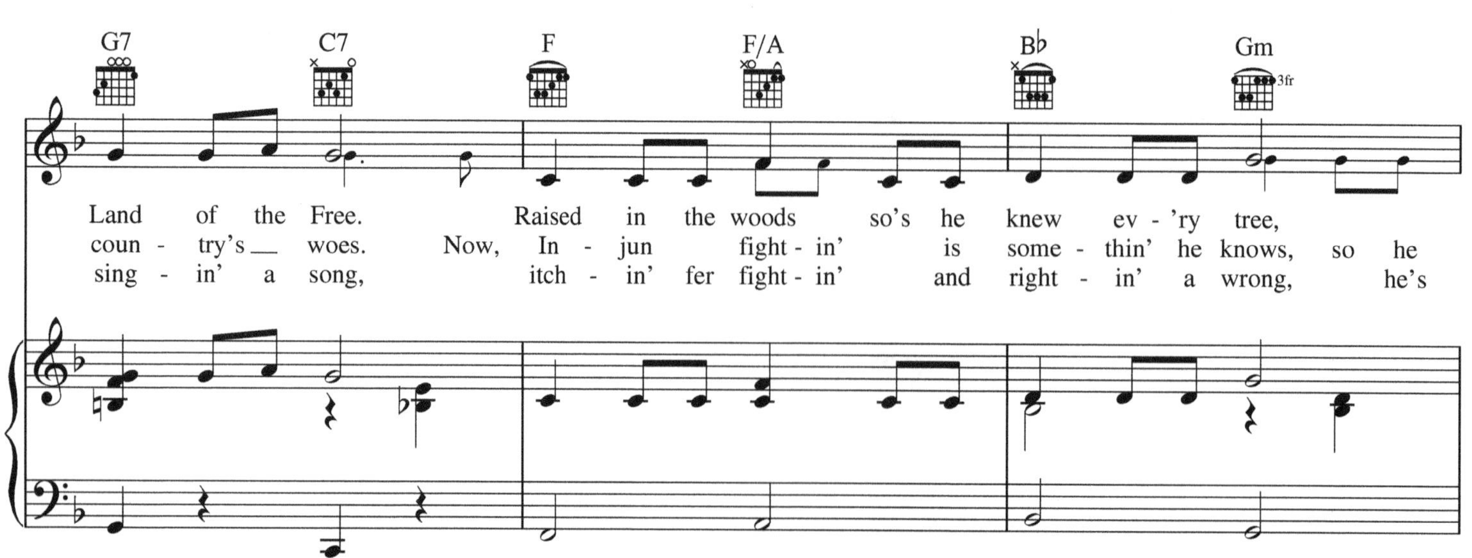

C7
F
kilt him a b'ar when he was on - ly three. Da - vy,
shoul - ders his ri - fle, an' off he goes. Da - vy,
rin - gy as a b'ar, an' twict as strong. Da - vy.
B♭
F
C7
1 - 9
F
Da - vy Crock - ett, king of the wild fron - tier! 2. In
Da - vy Crock - ett, man who don't know fear!
Da - vy Crock - ett, buck - skin buc - ca - neer!
10
F
F
C7
F
B♭
F
fear!
11.-17. (See additional lyrics)
18. he come home his pol - i - tick - in' done, the
19. heard of Hous - ton an' Aus - tin, an', so,
20. land is big - gest an' his land is best, from

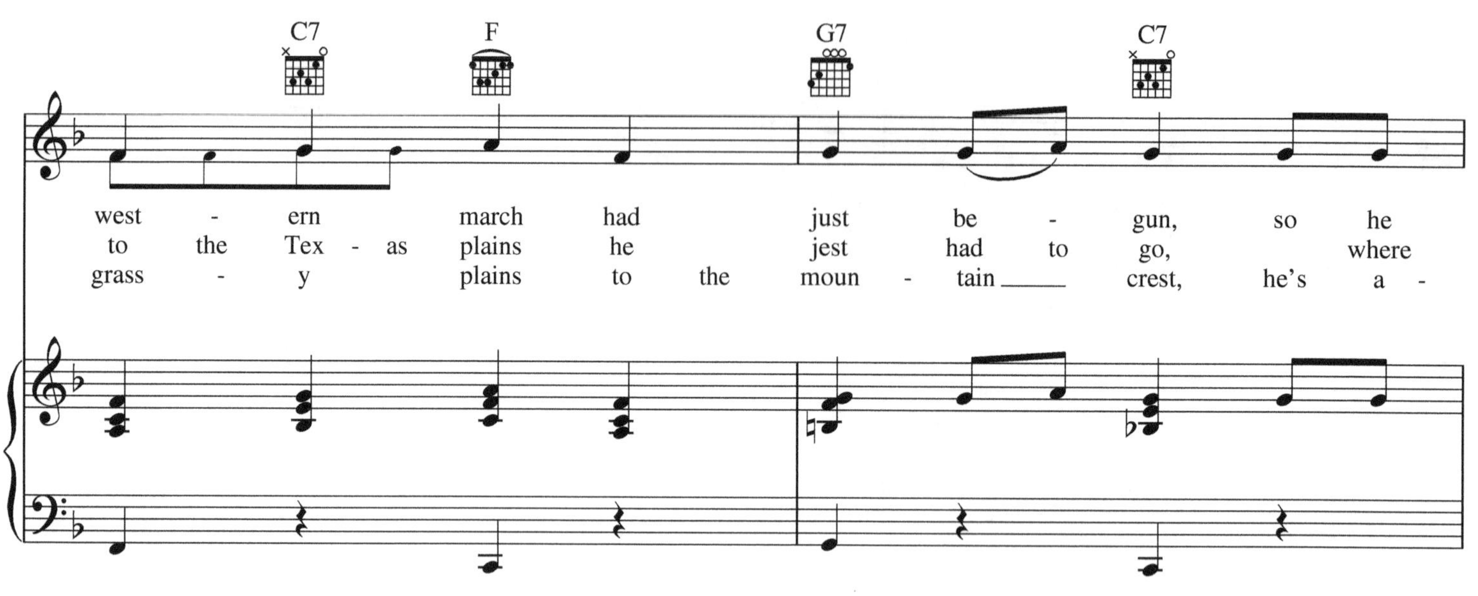
C7 F G7 C7
west - ern march had just be - gun, so he
to the Tex - as plains he jest had to go, where
grass - y plains to the moun - tain crest, he's a -

F F/A B♭ Gm 3fr C7
packed his gear an' his trust - y gun, an' lit out grin - nin' to
Free - dom was fight - in' an - oth - er foe, an' they need - ed him at the
head of us all meet - in' the test, fol - low - in' his leg - end

F B♭ F
fol - low the sun. Da - vy, Da - vy Crock - ett,
Al - a - mo. Da - vy, Da - vy Crock - ett,
in - to the West. Da - vy, Da - vy Crock - ett, the

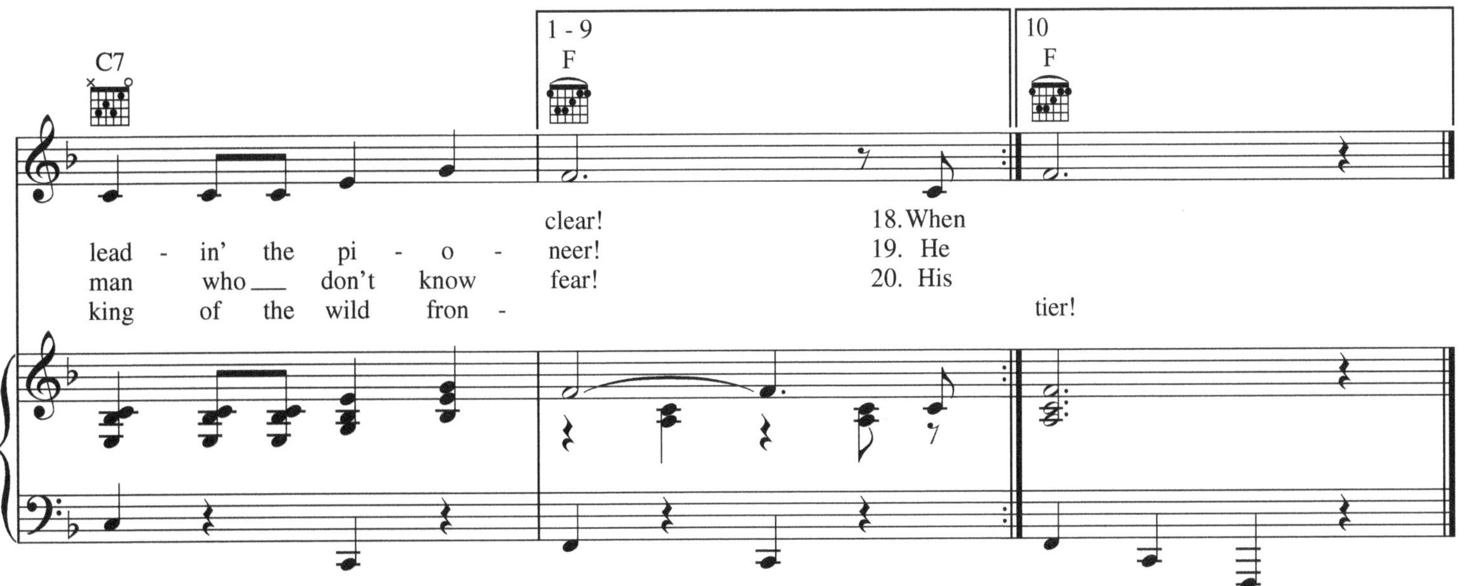

Additional Lyrics

4. Andy Jackson is our gen'ral's name,
His reg'lar soldiers we'll put to shame,
Them redskin varmints us Volunteers'll tame,
'Cause we got the guns with the sure-fire aim.
Davy – Davy Crockett,
The champion of us all!

5. Headed back to war from the ol' home place,
But Red Stick was leadin' a merry chase,
Fightin' an' burnin' at a devil's pace
South to the swamps on the Florida Trace.
Davy – Davy Crockett,
Trackin' the redskins down!

6. Fought single-handed through the Injun War
Till the Creeks was whipped an' peace was in store,
An' while he was handlin' this risky chore,
Made hisself a legend forevermore.
Davy – Davy Crockett,
King of the wild frontier!

7. He give his word an' he give his hand
That his Injun friends could keep their land,
An' the rest of his life he took the stand
That justice was due every redskin band.
Davy – Davy Crockett,
Holdin' his promise dear!

8. Home fer the winter with his family,
Happy as squirrels in the ol' gum tree,
Bein' the father he wanted to be,
Close to his boys as the pod an' the pea.
Davy – Davy Crockett,
Holdin' his young 'uns dear!

9. But the ice went out an' the warm winds came
An' the meltin' snow showed tracks of game,
An' the flowers of Spring filled the woods with flame,
An' all of a sudden life got too tame.
Davy – Davy Crockett,
Headin' on West again!

10. Off through the woods we're ridin' along,
Makin' up yarns an' singin' a song.
He's ringy as a b'ar and twice as strong,
An' knows he's right 'cause he ain't often wrong.
Davy – Davy Crockett,
The man who don't know fear!

11. Lookin' fer a place where the air smells clean,
Where the tree is tall an' the grass is green,
Where the fish is fat in an untouched stream,
An' the teemin' woods is a hunter's dream.
Davy – Davy Crockett,
Lookin' fer Paradise!

12. Now he'd lost his love an' his grief was gall.
In his heart he wanted to leave it all,
An' lose himself in the forests tall,
But he answered instead his country's call.
Davy – Davy Crockett,
Beginnin' his campaign!

13. Needin' his help they didn't vote blind,
They put in Davy 'cause he was their kind,
Sent up to Nashville the best they could find,
A fightin' spirit an' a thinkin' mind.
Davy – Davy Crockett,
Choice of the whole frontier!

14. The votes were counted an' he won hands down,
So they sent him off to Washin'ton town
With his best dress suit still his buckskins brown,
A livin' legend of growin' renown.
Davy – Davy Crockett,
The Canebrake Congressman!

15. He went off to Congress an' served a spell,
Fixin' up the Gover'ment an' laws as well,
Took over Washin'ton so we heered tell
An' patched up the crack in the Liberty Bell.
Davy – Davy Crockett,
Seein' his duty clear!

16. Him an' his jokes travelled all through the land,
An' his speeches made him friends to beat the band,
His politickin' was their favorite brand
An' everyone wanted to shake his hand.
Davy – Davy Crockett,
Helpin' his legend grow!

17. He knew when he spoke he sounded the knell
Of his hopes for White House an' fame as well,
But he spoke out strong so hist'ry books tell
An' patched up the crack in the Liberty Bell.
Davy – Davy Crockett,
Seein' his duty clear!

CHATTANOOGIE SHOE SHINE BOY

G7
C
boo - gie woo - gie rag, the Chat - ta - noo - gie shoe shine boy.
G6
C
C7
He charg - es you a nick - el just to shine one shoe, he
C
C7
F7
makes the old - est kind of leath - er look like new. You feel as though you want to dance when
C
he gets through, he's a great big bun - dle of joy. He pops a

G7
C
boo - gie woo - gie rag, the Chat - ta - noo - gie shoe shine boy.
C7
F
C
It's a won - der that the rag don't tear the way he makes it pop.
D7
You ought to see him fan the air with his
G7
N.C.
G6
C
hop - pi - ty hip - pi - ty, hip - pi - ty hop - pi - ty, hop - pi - ty hip - pi - ty hop. He o - pens up for bus' - ness when the

C7
C
C7
clock strikes nine, he likes to get 'em ear - ly when they're feel - in' fine.
F7
C
Ev - 'ry - bod - y gets a lit - tle rise and shine with the great big bun - dle of joy.
G7
C
He pops a boo - gie woo - gie rag, the Chat - ta - noo - gie shoe shine boy.
1
G
2
Have you

COLD, COLD HEART

Words and Music by
HANK WILLIAMS

F7
B♭
lone - some past keeps us so far a - part. Why
hide from life? To try it just ain't smart. Why
C7
can't I free your doubt - ful mind and melt your cold, cold
can't I free your doubt - ful mind and melt your cold, cold
F
heart? An - oth - er love be - fore my time made your heart sad and
heart? There was a time when I be - lieved that you be - longed to
C7
blue, and so my heart is pay - ing now for
me, but now I know your heart is shack - led

F
things I didn't do. In anger, unkind
to a memory. The more I learn to
F7
Bb
words are said that make the teardrops start. Why
care for you, the more we drift apart. Why
C7
1
can't I free your doubtful mind and melt your cold, cold
can't I free your doubtful mind and
F
2
F
heart? You'll melt your cold, cold heart?

DON'T LET THE STARS GET IN YOUR EYES

Words and Music by
SLIM WILLET

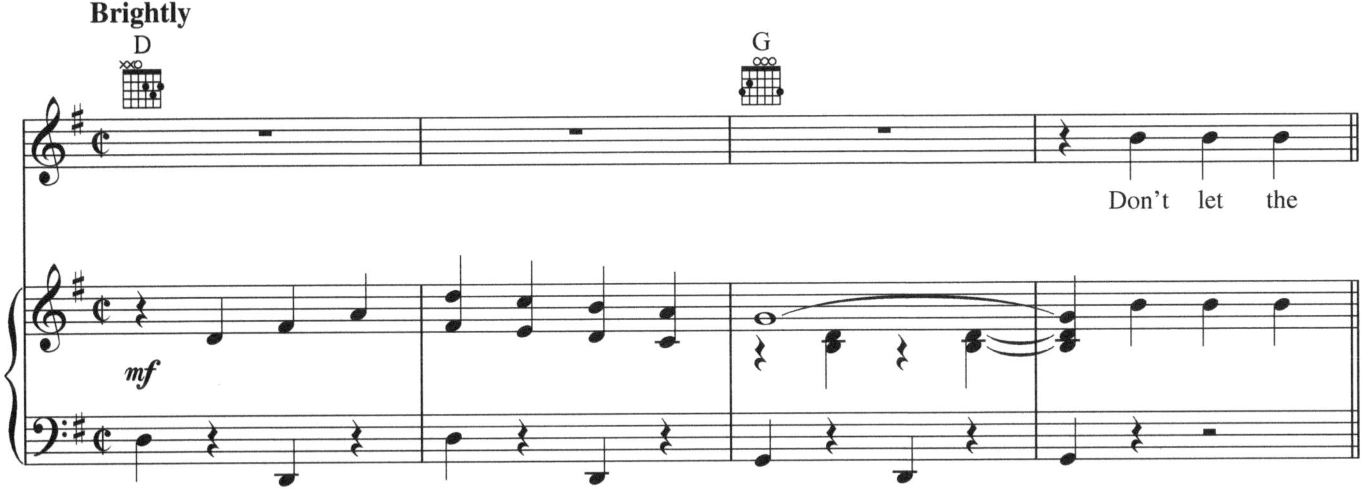

G
dies; don't let the stars get in your eyes. Oh, keep your heart for me, for
D7
To Coda
some - day I'll re - turn and you know you're the on - ly one I'll ev - er
G
love.
Too man - y nights, too man - y
Too man - y miles, too man - y
stars, too man - y moons could change your
days, too man - y nights to be a -

D7
mind.
lone.
If I'm gone too long, don't for -
Oh, please keep your heart
get where you be - long; when the stars come out, re - mem - ber you are
while we're a - part; don't lin - ger in the moon - light while I'm
1
G
mine.
Don't let the
2
G
gone.
D.S. al Coda
Don't let the
CODA
G
love.

CRAZY ARMS

Words and Music by RALPH MOONEY
and CHARLES SEALS

F
B♭
F
F7
B♭
mine.
time.
Cra - zy arms that reach to hold some-bod - y
F
C7
new, but my yearn-ing heart keeps say - ing you're not mine.
My
F
F7
B♭
F
trou - bled mind knows soon to an - oth - er you'll be wed, and that's why I'm
C7
1
F
B♭7
F
C7
2
F
B♭7
F
lone - ly all the time.
time.

EL PASO

Words and Music by
MARTY ROBBINS

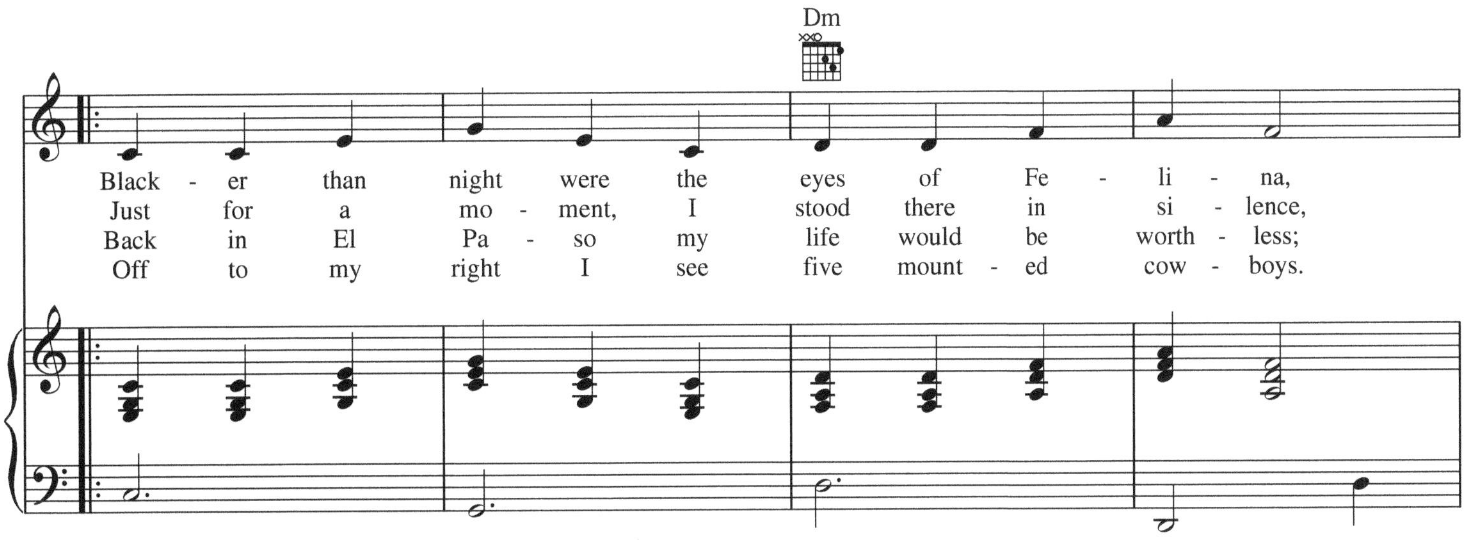
Dm
Black - er than night were the eyes of Fe - li - na,
Just for a mo - ment, I stood there in si - lence,
Back in El Pa - so my life would be worth - less;
Off to my right I see five mount - ed cow - boys.

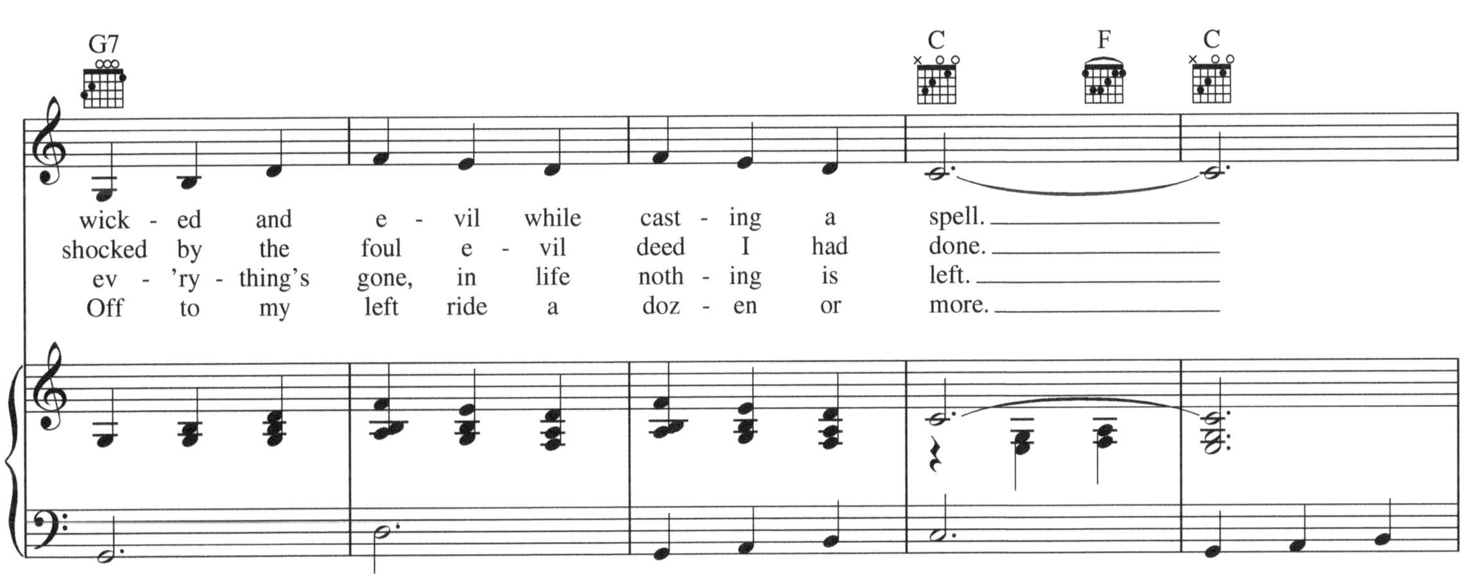
G7
C
F
C
wick - ed and e - vil while cast - ing a spell.
shocked by the foul e - vil deed I had done.
ev - 'ry - thing's gone, in life noth - ing is left.
Off to my left ride a doz - en or more.

Dm
My love was deep for this Mex - i - can maid - en.
Man - y thoughts raced through my mind as I stood there.
It's been so long since I've seen the young maid - en.
Shout - ing and shoot - ing, I can't let them catch me.

G7
C
F
C
I was in love, but in vain, I could tell.
I had but one chance, and that was to run.
My love is strong - er than my fear of death.
I have to make it to Ro - sa's back door.

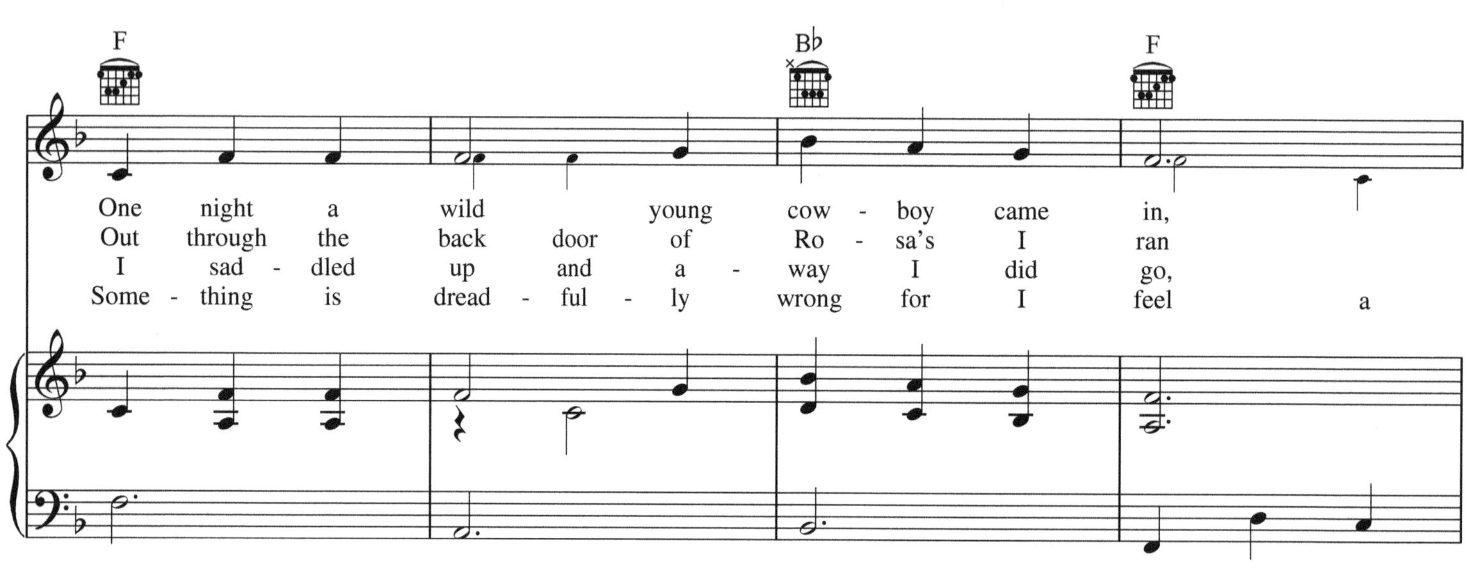
F
B♭
F
One night a wild young cow - boy came in,
Out through the back door of Ro - sa's I ran
I sad - dled up and a - way I did go,
Some - thing is dread - ful - ly wrong for I feel a

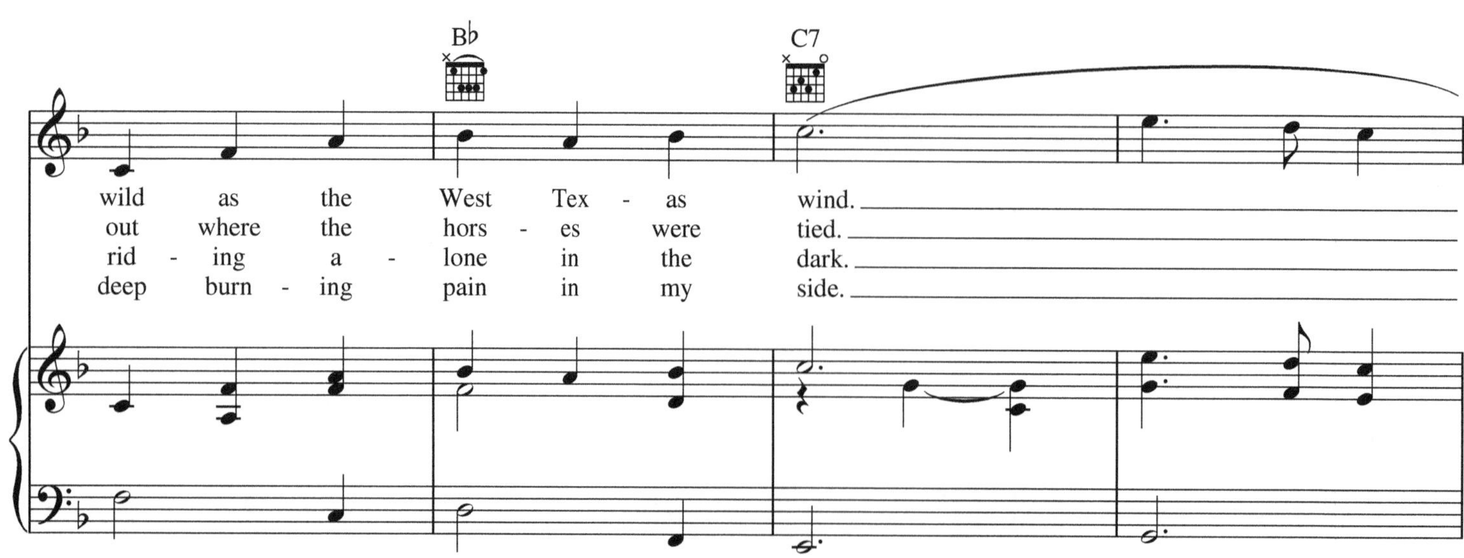
B♭
C7
wild as the West Tex - as wind.
out where the hors - es were tied.
rid - ing a - lone in the dark.
deep burn - ing pain in my side.

Dash - ing and dar - ing, a
I caught a good one, it
May - be to - mor - row a
Though I am try - ing to

drink he was shar - ing with wick - ed Fe - li - na, the
looked like it could run. Up on its back and a -
bul - let will find me. To - night, noth - ing's worse than this
stay in the sad - dle, I'm get - ting wear - y, un -

F
G
G7
girl that I loved. So, in an - ger, I
way I did ride just as fast as I
pain in my heart. And at last, here I
a - ble to ride. But my love for Fe -

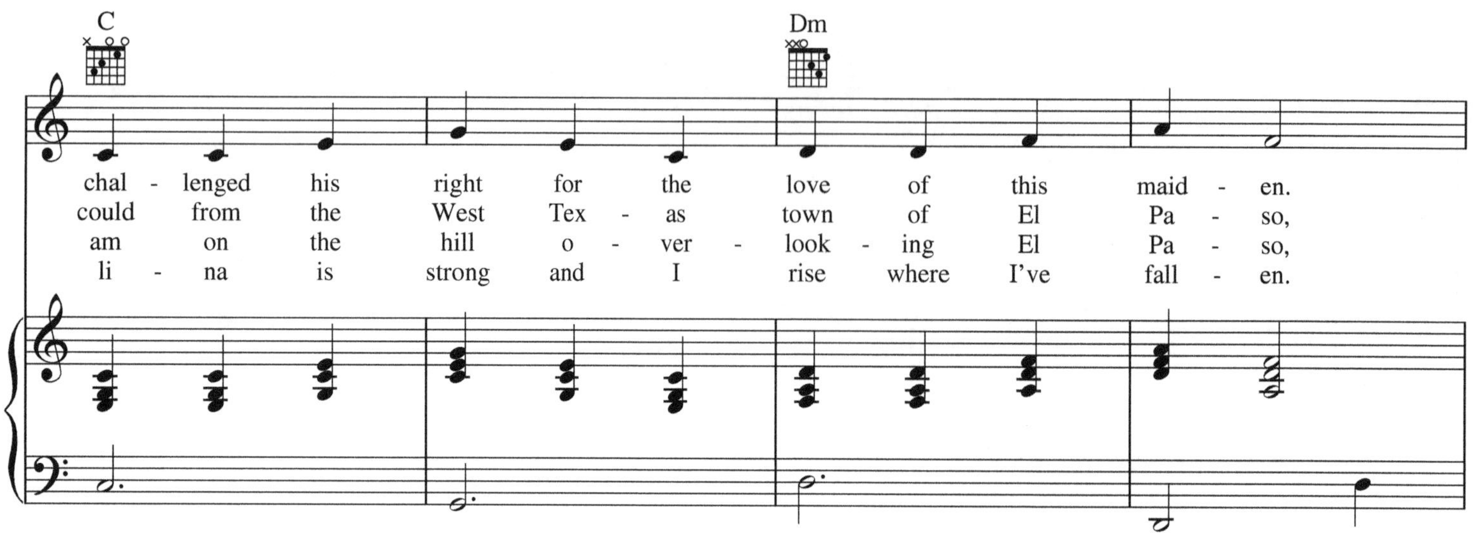
C
Dm
chal - lenged his right for the love of this maid - en.
could from the West Tex - as town of El Pa - so,
am on the hill o - ver - look - ing El Pa - so,
li - na is strong and I rise where I've fall - en.

G7
C
F
Down went his hand for the gun that he wore.
out to the bad - lands of New Mex - i - co.
I can see Ro - sa's Can - ti - na be - low.
Though I am wear - y, I can't stop to rest.

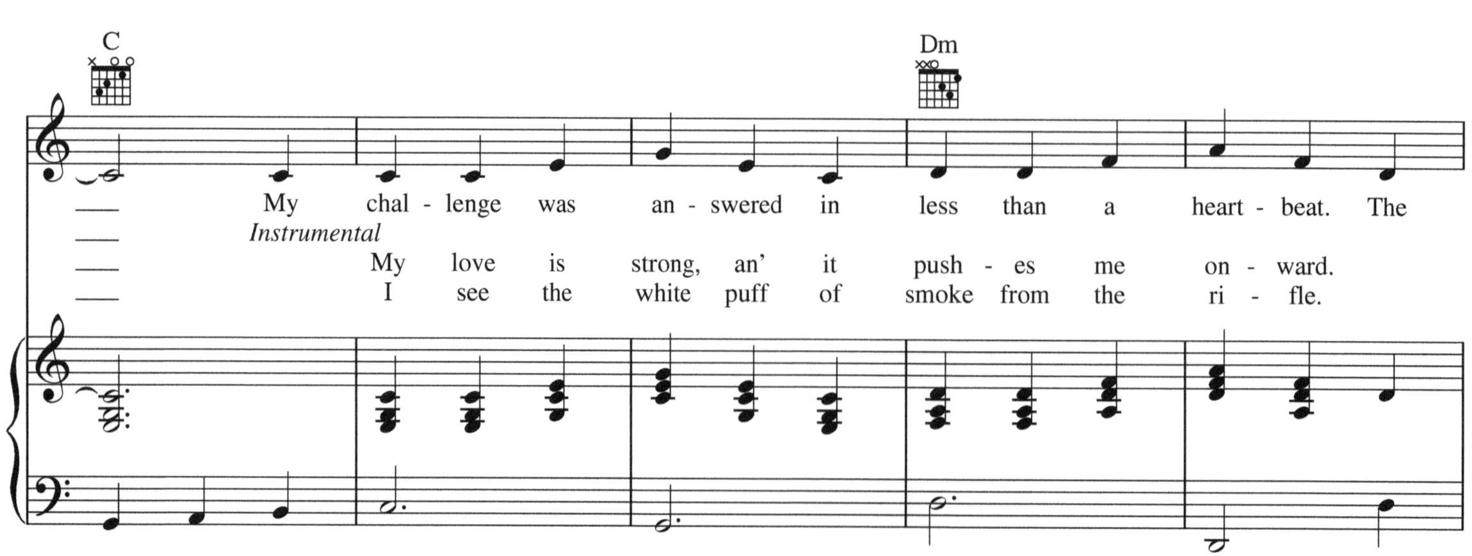
C
Dm
My chal - lenge was an - swered in less than a heart - beat. The
Instrumental
My love is strong, an' it push - es me on - ward.
I see the white puff of smoke from the ri - fle.

G7
C
F
C
Play 4 times
hand - some young stran - ger lay dead on the floor.
Instrumental ends
Down off the hill to Fe - li - na I go.
I feel the bul - let go deep in my chest.
Dm
From out of no - where, Fe - li - na has found me,
Cra - dled by two lov - ing arms that I'll die for,
G7
1
C
F
C
kiss - ing my cheek as she kneels by my side.
one lit - tle kiss, then Fe - li - na, good -
2
C
F
C
bye.

FOUR WALLS

Words and Music by MARVIN J. MOORE
and GEORGE H. CAMPBELL, JR.

Am7
D7
Four walls to hear me, four
G
G7
walls to see. Four walls too
C
G
D7
G
near me, clos - ing in on me.
1, 2
3
G
D7
G
Clos - ing in on me.
rall.

FULL TIME JOB

Words and Music by
GERALD TEIFER

C9
G6
E7
have no plan to use a full time man, a
A7
D7
part time job will do. I want a
G6
life - time job be - ing close to you,
C9
G6
mak - ing all your dreams come true. But if your

C9
G6
E7
heart don't throb a - bout a full time job, a
A7
D7
G6
part time job will do.
Solo ends
You
C9
would - n't have to pay me a
G
D9
4fr
G6
nick - el or a dime, as

C9
long as you would let me get in a
G6
G♯dim7
D7
G
lit - tle bit of o - ver - time. I want a full time job
hold - ing hands with you.
C7
I think you'd kind - a like it,
G
C7
G
too. Don't need a part time job, I want a full time

1
E7
A7
D7
G6
job, but a part time job will do.
2
C9
G6
E7
A7
D7
3
3
G6

GONE

Words and Music by
SMOKEY ROGERS

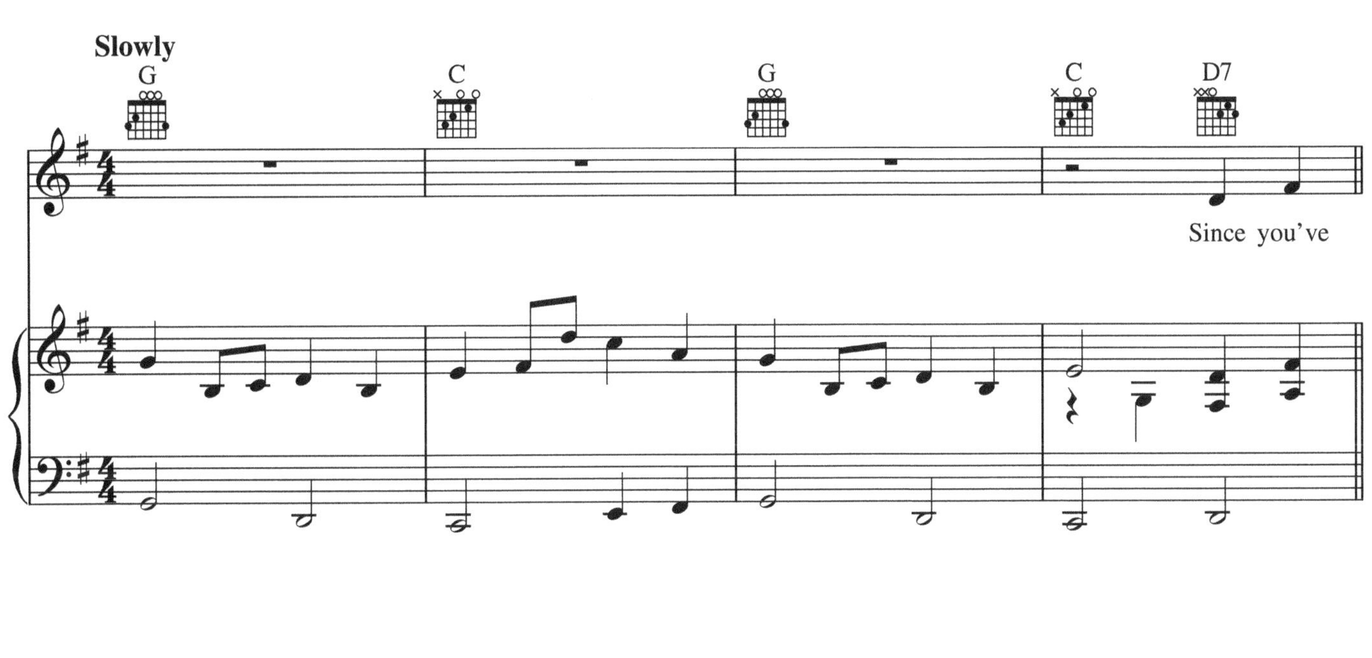

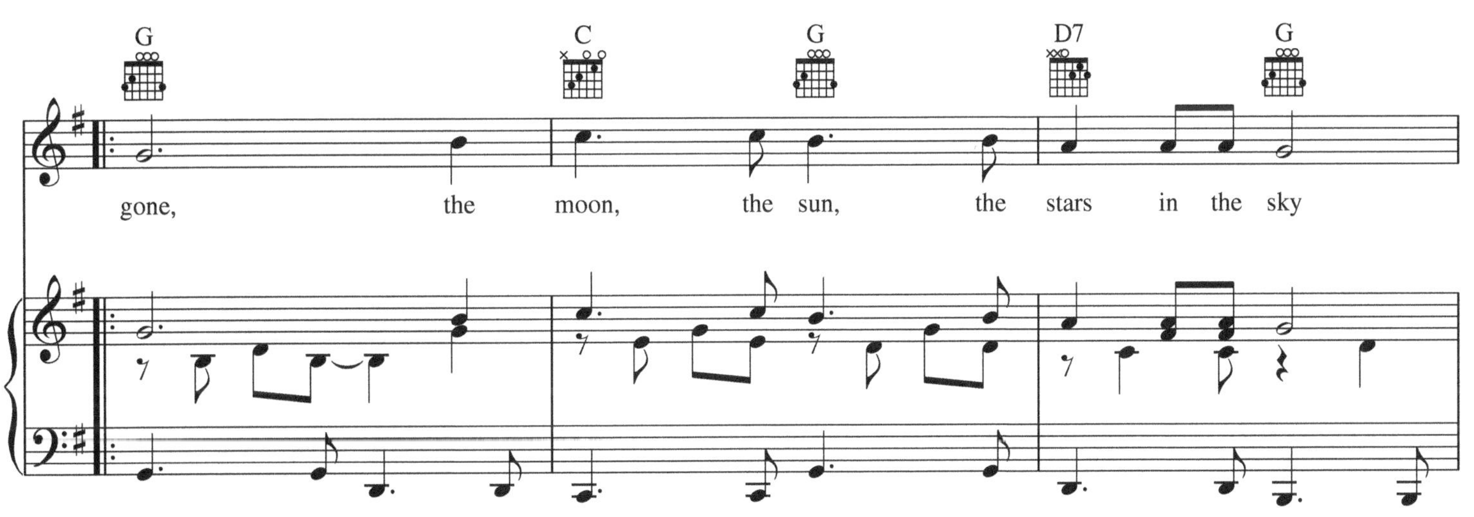

D7
G
C
once was mine. Now you've gone.
Since you've gone, my heart, my lips, my
tear - dimmed eyes, a lone - ly soul with - in me cries. I
act - ed smart, broke your heart. Now you've

G
C
G
N.C.
D7
gone.
Oh.
What I'd
give for the life - time I've wast - ed,
the
love that I've tast - ed. I was wrong. Now you've
gonc.
Since you've
gone.
1
2

GOLDEN ROCKET

Words and Music by
HANK SNOW

F/A
F/E
F7/E♭
You dealt the cards but you missed a play, so
I'm tired of run - nin' on the same old track, bought a
This mid - night spe - cial is a - burn - in' the rail, so
Now from your call - board e - rase my name. Your
The brake - man start - ed sing - in' a song, said, "You're
When I kissed my ba - by at the sta - tion door, that
B♭
F
C7
hit the road and be on your way. Gon-na board the Gold - en Rock - et and leave this
one - way tick - et and I won't be back. This Gold - en Rock - et's gon - na roll my blues a -
wom - an, don't try to fol - low my trail. This Gold - en Rock - et's gon - na roll my blues a -
fire went out, you done lost your flame, and this Gold - en Rock - et is roll - in' my blues a -
wor - ried now but it won't be long. This Gold - en Rock - et is leav - in' your blues be -
whis - tle blow, like it nev - er be - fore, of the Gold - en Rock - et that rolled my blues a -
1-5
F
B♭
F
Gm7
C7
6
F
B♭
F
Gm7
F
town. I
way.
way.
way. That
hind." Then the
way.

HEARTACHES BY THE NUMBER

Words and Music by
HARLAN HOWARD

F7
B♭
N.C.
you came back and nev - er meant to stay.
wait - ed but you must have lost your way.
Now I've got
B♭
E♭
3fr
heart - aches by the num - ber, trou - bles by the score.
F7
Ev - 'ry day you love me less, each day I love you
B♭
N.C.
B♭
more. Yes, I've got heart - aches by the

Eb
3fr
num - ber, a love that I can't win, but the
F7
day that I stop count - ing, that's the
1
day my world will
Bb
end.
2
day my
world will
Bb
end.

HEARTBREAK HOTEL

Words and Music by MAE BOREN AXTON,
TOMMY DURDEN and ELVIS PRESLEY

though it's al - ways crowd-ed, you still can find _ some room for bro-ken-heart - ed lov - ers _ to
cry a - way _ their gloom. They'll be so, they'll be just so lone - ly, ba - by,
A7
they'll be just so lone - ly, they'll be so lone - ly _ they could die. Now the
B7
E
bell-hop's tears keep flow - ing; the desk clerk's _ dressed in black. Well, they've

been so long on Lone - ly Street they'll nev - er, they'll nev - er look ba - ack, and the - ey're so,
well, they're just so lone - ly, ba - by, well, they're so lone - ly,
well, they're so lone - ly they could die. Well now, if your ba - by leaves you, you've
got a tale to tell. Well, just take a walk down Lone - ly Street to

Heart - break Ho - tel where you will be, will be just so lone - ly, ba - by,

well, you'll be lone - ly. You'll be so lone - ly you could die.

A9
5fr
Piano solo ad lib.

B7
E
Al - though it's al - ways crowd - ed, well, you
still can find some room for bro - ken - heart - ed lov - ers to
A7
cry a - way their gloom. They'll be so, well, they'll get so lone - ly, ba - by, well, they're so lone - ly,
B7
E
Fmaj7 Emaj7
they'll be so lone - ly they could die.

HEY, GOOD LOOKIN'

Words and Music by
HANK WILLIAMS

C
Hey, sweet ba - by, don't you think may - be
No more look - in', I know I've been took - en.
D7
G7
C
we could find us a brand - new rec - i - pe?
How's a - bout keep - in' stead - y com - pa - ny?
C7
F
C
I got a hot rod Ford and a two dol - lar bill and
I'm gon - na throw my date book o - ver the fence and
F
C
F
I know a spot right o - ver the hill. There's so - da pop and the
find me one for five or ten cents. I'll keep it 'til it's

D7
G7
danc - in's free, so if you wan - na have fun come a - long with me.
cov - ered with age 'cause I'm writ - in' your name down on ev - 'ry page.
C
Hey, good look - in', what - cha got cook - in'?
D7
G7
1
C
How's a - bout cook - in' some - thin' up with me?
Dm
G7
I'm
2
C
F
C
C6
me?

HEY JOE!

Words and Music by
BOUDLEAUX BRYANT

Hey, Joe, she's got skin that's
Hey Joe, quit that wait - in',
cream - y dream - y, eyes that look so love - y, dove - y, lips as red as cher - ry, ber - ry
hes - i - tat - in'. Let me at 'er, what's the mat - ter? You're as slow as an - y Joe can
Eb Eb7 Ab Eb7 Ab
3fr 4fr 4fr
wine. Now, lis - ten, Joe, I'm not a heel.
be. Now, come on, Joe, let's make a deal.
Eb7 Ab Eb7 Ab Eb7 Ab
4fr 4fr 4fr
But old bud - dy, let me tell you how I feel. She's a hon - ey, she's a
Let me dance with her to see if she is real. She's the cut - est girl I've

A
B♭7
sug - ar - pie. I'm warn-ing you I'm gon - na try to steal her from you.
ev - er seen. I'll tell you face to face I mean to steal her from you.
E♭
3fr
Hey Joe, though we've been the
Hey Joe, we'll be friends un -
A♭
4fr
B♭7
B♭dim7
best of friends, this is where that friend - ship ends. I've got - ta have that
til the end, but this looks like the end, my friend. I've got - ta have that
B♭7
1
E♭
3fr
B♭7
2
E♭
3fr
dol - ly for my own.
dol - ly for my
own.
8vb

I CAN'T STOP LOVING YOU

Words and Music by
DON GIBSON

C
C7
F
time heals a bro - ken heart,
C
G7
C
F/G
but time has stood still since we've been a - part.
C
C7
F
I can't stop lov - ing you, so I've made up my
I can't stop lov - ing you, there's no use to
3
C
G7
mind to live in mem - o - ry
try. Pre - tend there's some - one new;

C
C7
of old lone - some times.
I can't stop
I can't live a lie.
I can't stop
F
C
want - ing you,
it's use - less to say,
want - ing you
the way that I do.
3
G7
so I'll just live my life in dreams of yes - ter -
There's on - ly been one love for me, that one love is
1
C
F/G
C
G7
day.
Those hap - py
2
C
F
C
you.

I WANT TO BE WITH YOU ALWAYS

Words and Music by JIM BECK
and LEFTY FRIZZELL

B♭7
E♭
3fr
But when I'm gone, and I'm all a-
Then we'd trav-el far to some big shin-in'
'Cause my love is true, my love is on-ly for
B♭
F7
To Coda
lone, I'll be sing-in' this song.
star, just you and my gui-tar,
you. I'll nev-er be blue,
B♭
F7
I wan-na be with you al-ways.
and stay there, sweet-heart, for al-ways.
B♭
F7

B♭
E♭
3fr
3
B♭
F7
B♭
1
2
D.S. al Coda
I'd be hap-py,
I hope you feel the
CODA
F7
N.C.
3
A
B♭6
if I can be with you al - ways.
rit.

I WALK THE LINE

Words and Music by
JOHN R. CASH

Additional Lyrics

3. As sure as night is dark and day is light,
   I keep you on my mind both day and night.
   And happiness I've known proves that it's right.
   Because you're mine I walk the line.

4. You've got a way to keep me on your side.
   You give me cause for love that I can't hide.
   For you I know I'd even try to turn the tide.
   Because you're mine I walk the line.

5. I keep a close watch on this heart of mine.
   I keep my eyes wide open all the time.
   I keep the ends out for the tie that binds.
   Because you're mine I walk the line.

I'M MOVIN' ON

Words and Music by
HANK SNOW

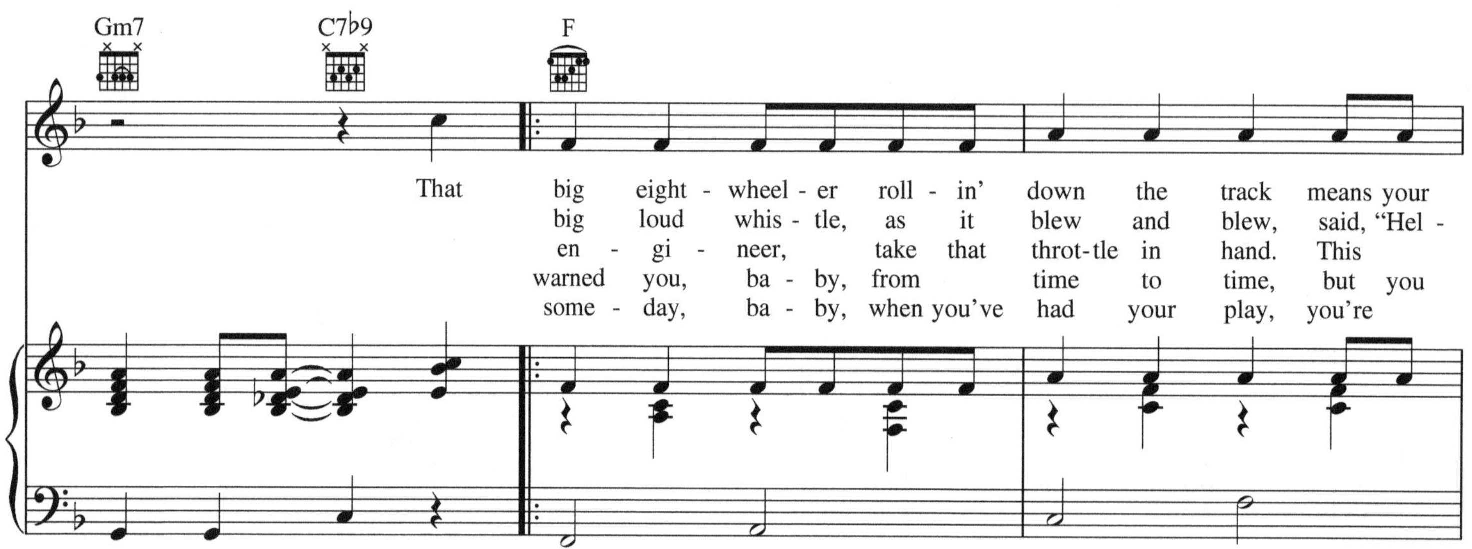

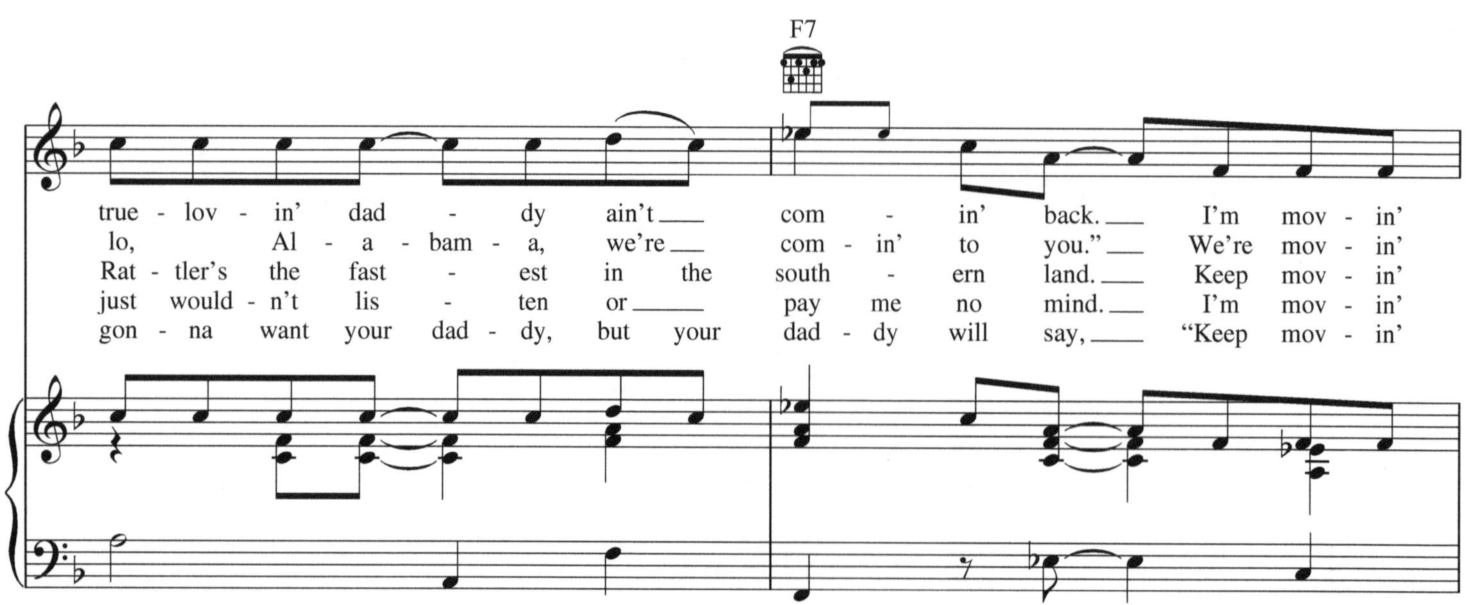

B♭
F
on. I'll soon be gone.
on. Oh, hear my song.
on. Keep roll - in' on.
on. I'm roll - in' on.
on. You stayed a - way too long."
C7
You were fly - in' too high for my lit - tle old sky, so I'm mov - in'
You had the laugh on me, so I've set you free, and I'm mov - in'
You're gon - na ease my mind, so put me there on time. Keep roll - in'
You have bro - ken your vow and it's all o - ver now, so I'm mov - in'
I'm through with you, too bad you are blue, so keep mov - in'
F
1-4
B♭
C7
5
on. That
on. Mis - ter
on. I
on. But
on.

IN THE JAILHOUSE NOW

Words and Music by
JIMMIE RODGERS

A7
Dm
A7
Mon - day that Bob got locked up Sun - day. They
mon - ey. She start-ed in - to call me "Hon - ey." We
D7
Am7
D7
G7
Dm7
got him in the jail - house way down - town.
took in ev - 'ry hon - ky - tonk in town.
G7
C
C7
He's in the jail-house now. He's in the jail-house now.
We're in the jail-house now. We're in the jail-house now.
F
G7
I told him once or
They told us once or

To Coda
Dm7
G7
Gdim7
G7
twice to quit play - in' cards and shoot - in' dice.
twice to quit play - in' cards and
He's in the jail-house now.
C
D.S. al Coda
Well,
CODA
G7
shoot - in' dice. We're in the
G7♯5
C
F
C
F
C
jail - house now.

IT WASN'T GOD WHO MADE HONKY TONK ANGELS

Words and Music by
J.D. MILLER

E♭
E♭7
A♭
lis - ten to the words you are say - ing,
start most ev - 'ry heart that's ev - er bro - ken
B♭7
it brings mem - 'ries when I was a trust - ing
was be - cause there al - ways was a man to
E♭
Fm7
E♭/G
B♭7
Adim7/B♭
E♭
wife.
blame.
It was - n't God who made
Fm
E♭7/G
A♭
hon - ky tonk an - gels,
as you

B♭7
E♭
3fr
B♭7 Adim7/B♭
said in the words of your song.
Too man - y
E♭
3fr
Fm
E♭7/G
A♭
4fr
times mar - ried men think they're still sin - gle;
B♭7
that has caused man - y a good girl to go
1
E♭
3fr
F7
B♭7
wrong.
It's a
2
E♭
3fr
A♭6
3fr
E♭
3fr
wrong.

JAMBALAYA
(On the Bayou)

Words and Music by
HANK WILLIAMS

G7
vonne, the sweet - est one, me oh my oh. Son of a
style and go hog - wild, me oh my oh. Son of a
mon to buy Y - vonne what we need - o. Son of a
C
gun, we'll have big fun on the bay - ou.
gun, we'll have big fun on the bay - ou.
gun, we'll have big fun on the bay - ou.
Jam - ba - la - ya and a craw - fish pie and fil - let
G7
gum - bo, 'cause to - night I'm gon - na

C
see my ma cher a - mi - o.
Pick gui -
G7
tar, fill fruit jar and be gay - o.
Son of a
1, 2
C
gun, we'll have big fun on the bay - ou.
3
C
Thi - bo -
Set - tle
bay - ou.
rit.

MAKING BELIEVE

Words and Music by
JIMMY WORK

B♭
F
dream, still I'll nev - er own you.
fu - ture will nev - er come true.
C7
F
Mak - ing be - lieve, it's all I can do.
Mak - ing be - lieve, what else can I do?
C7
Can't hold you close when you're not
F
C7
with me. You're some - bod - y's love,

F
you'll nev - er be mine.
Mak - ing be - lieve
B♭
F
I'll spend my life - time lov - ing
C7
you, mak - ing be - lieve.
1
F
B♭
F
Mak - ing be - lieve.
2
F
rit.

KENTUCKY WALTZ

Words and Music by
BILL MONROE

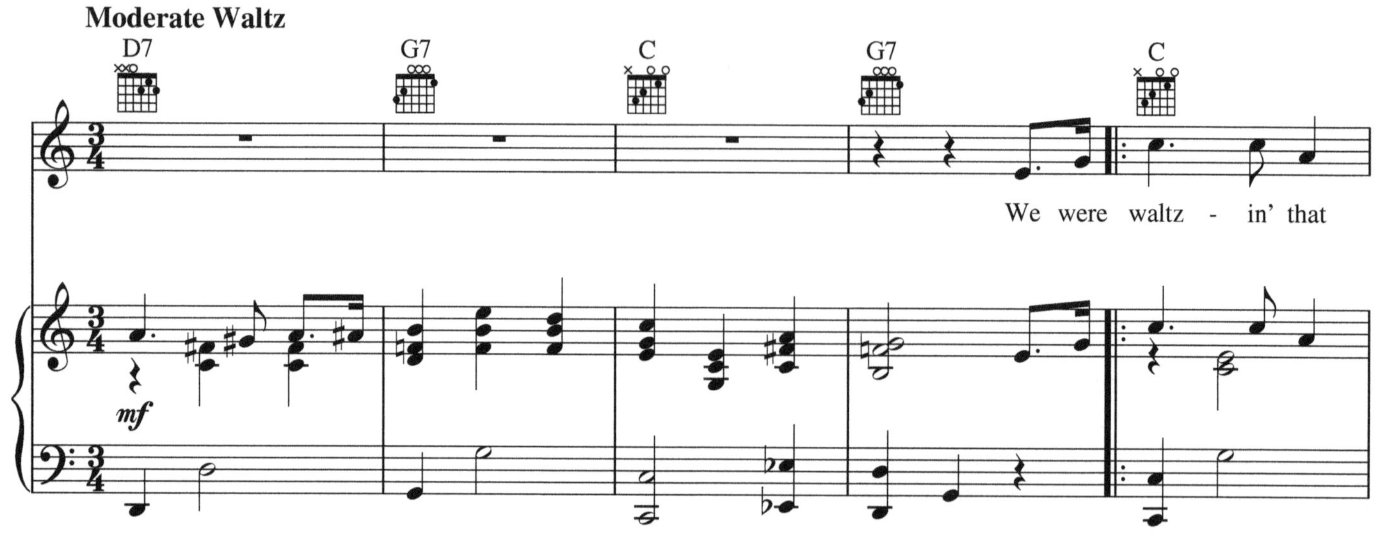

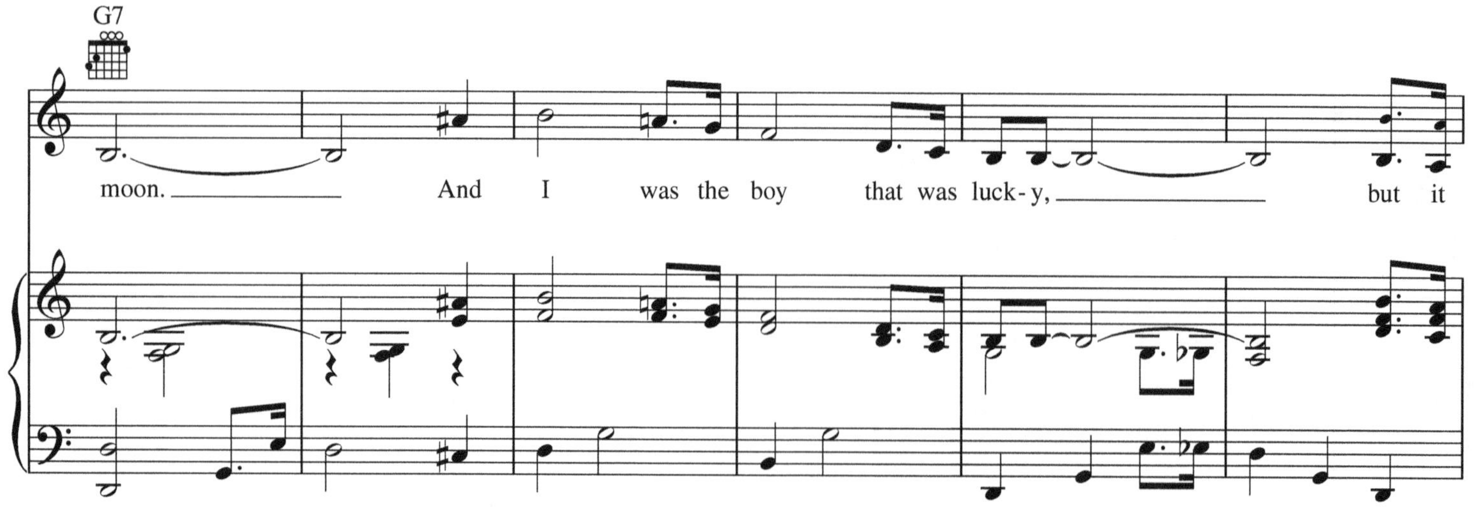

C
all ended too soon. As I sit here a-
C7
F
lone in the moon-light, I see your smil-ing face.
C
A7
And I long once more for your em-brace and that
D7
G7
1
C
G7
2
C
beau-ti-ful Ken-tuck-y Waltz. We were Waltz.
poco rit.

LOVE, LOVE, LOVE

Words and Music by
TED JARRETT

A
E
you're still my ba - by.
tell ev - 'ry - bod - y,
I want the whole world to know I just
B
E
love, love, love, love, love you, love you so.
A
E
Friends'll try to tell me that I'm just a fool. Your love don't mean a thing. But
A
F♯
I'll keep hop - in' some-day that you'll see things my way. We'll make the wed - din' bells

B
N.C.
E
ring. Then I'll have you to keep me gay.
We'll be a - lone both night and day.
E7
A
So, tell ev - 'ry-bod - y, I want the
E
B7
whole world to know that I just love, love, love, love, love you, love you so.

E
To Coda
E7
A
E
A
F♯
B
N.C.
D.S. al Coda
Life's just too
CODA
I just
B
E
love, love, love, love, love you, love you so.

LOVE ME TENDER

Words and Music by ELVIS PRESLEY
and VERA MATSON

A7
D7sus
D7
G
life com - plete, and I love you so.
I be - long, and we'll nev - er part.
all the years till the end of time.
fol - low you ev - 'ry - where you go.
B7
Em
G7
C
Cm
3fr
Love me ten - der, love me true, all my dreams ful -
mf
G
Dm6/F
E7
A7
fill. For, my dar - lin', I love you,
1-3
D7sus
D7
G
C/D
D7
4
D7sus
D7
G
and I al - ways will. and I al - ways will.
rit.
mp

MOCKIN' BIRD HILL

Words and Music by
VAUGHN HORTON

C
heart fills with glad - ness when I hear the
tum - ble - down shack and a rust - y ol'
me and the sky and an ol' whip - poor -
D7
trill of the birds in the tree - tops on
mill, but it's my home, sweet home up on
will, sing - in' songs in the twi - light on
G
Mock - in' Bird Hill.
Mock - in' Bird Hill.
Mock - in' Bird Hill.
Tra - la la twit - tle - dee
3
3
mf
C
G
C
G
dee dee, it gives me a thrill to

D7
G
C
wake up in the morn - in' to the mock - in' bird's
G
C
G
trill. Tra - la la twit - tle - dee dee dee, there's
3
C
G
D7
peace and good will. You're wel - come as the
G
1, 2
3
flow - ers on Mock - in' Bird Hill.
Got a
When it's
Hill.

OH, LONESOME ME

Words and Music by
DON GIBSON

G7
1
C
2
C
Oh, lone-some me. A me.
G
D7
I'll bet she's not like me; she's out and fan - cy free,
G
flirt - ing with the boys with all her charms. But I still love her
D7
so and, broth - er, don't you know, I'd wel - come her right back here in my

G
G7
C
G7
arms. Well, there must be some way I can lose these lone-some blues.
C
For - get a - bout the past and find some - bod - y new. I've
C7
F
G7
thought of ev - 'ry - thing from A to Z. Oh,
C
G7
C
lone-some me.

MOM AND DAD'S WALTZ

Words and Music by
LEFTY FRIZZELL

F C G7 C
dad - dy. I want them to know I love them so.
dad - dy, be-cause I know I owe them my all.
G7 C
In my heart, joy tear starts 'cause I'm hap - py,
G7 C
and I pray ev - 'ry day for mom and pap - py. And each
G7 C G7 C
night I'd walk for miles, cry or smile for my ma - ma and

To Coda
F
C
G7
C
dad - dy. I want them to know I love them so.
3
3

G7
C

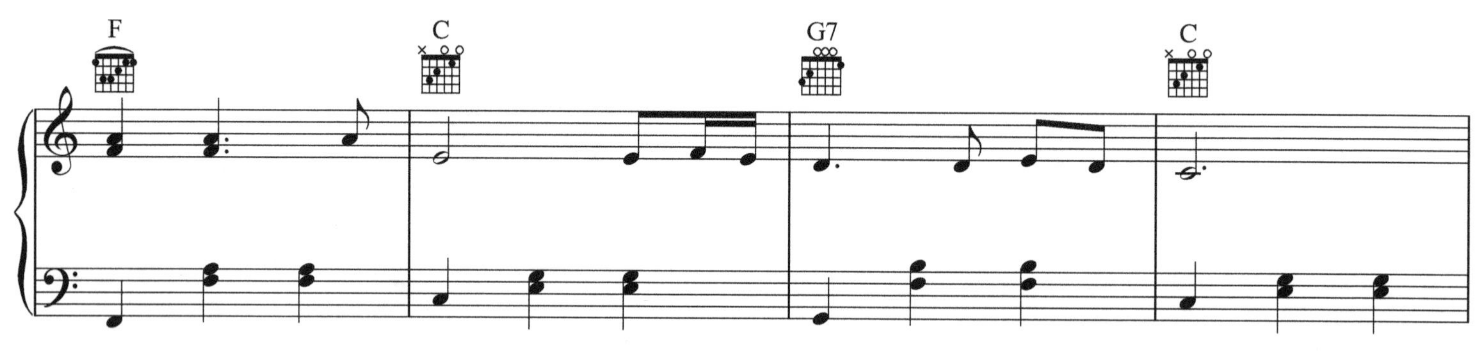
F
C
G7
C

G7
C

G7
C
G7
C
G7
C7
F
C
G7
C
D.S. al Coda
I'd fight in
CODA
C
G7
C
so.
I love them
3
so.
rit.
3

ONE BY ONE

Words and Music by JIM ANGLIN,
RICK ANGLIN and JOHNNIE WRIGHT

B♭7
E♭
3fr
To Coda
Both: We'll pay for our lies one by one.
A♭
4fr
E♭
3fr
Male: My plans and hopes have tum - bled down. My
B♭7
E♭
3fr
cas - tle of dreams plunged to the ground.
Female: How can you face
A♭
4fr
E♭
3fr
B♭7
me af - ter what you've done? You've shat - tered my dreams one by

E♭
3fr
D.S. al Coda
CODA
B♭7
one.
Both: One by
Ab
4fr
Male: How can you go to sleep at night?
love I treas-ured, you sold for gold.
Don't old mem-'ries make you long for day-light?
For world-ly goods you left me cold.
Female: You'll
Female: You're
pay the price af-ter hav-ing your fun.
hap-py now, but the time will come
You'll re-gret each mis-
your false lies will

B♭7
E♭
1
2
take _ one by one.
leave you one by one.
Male: The
Both: One by one we
A♭
E♭
broke each vow we made.
Female: It was you _ who lied, it was me who paid. _
B♭7
E♭
A♭
E♭
Male: As sure's there's a heav-en be-yond the sun, _
B♭7
E♭
Both: we'll pay _ for our lies _ one by one. _
3fr
4fr

POOR LITTLE FOOL

Words and Music by
SHARON SHEELEY

F
G7
C
Am
knew that I would fall,
heart was full of lies,
gave a - way my heart,
won her vic - to - ry,
fool - ish game with me,
poor lit - tle fool, oh yeah.
Dm7/F
G9
C
Am
I was a fool, uh - huh.
(Uh - huh, poor lit - tle fool.
F
To Coda
1-3
G
4
G
D.S. al Coda
I was a fool, oh yeah.)
She'd
She
The
yeah.)
Well, I've
CODA
G
C
yeah, oh yeah.)

RELEASE ME

Words and Music by ROBERT YOUNT,
EDDIE MILLER and DUB WILLIAMS

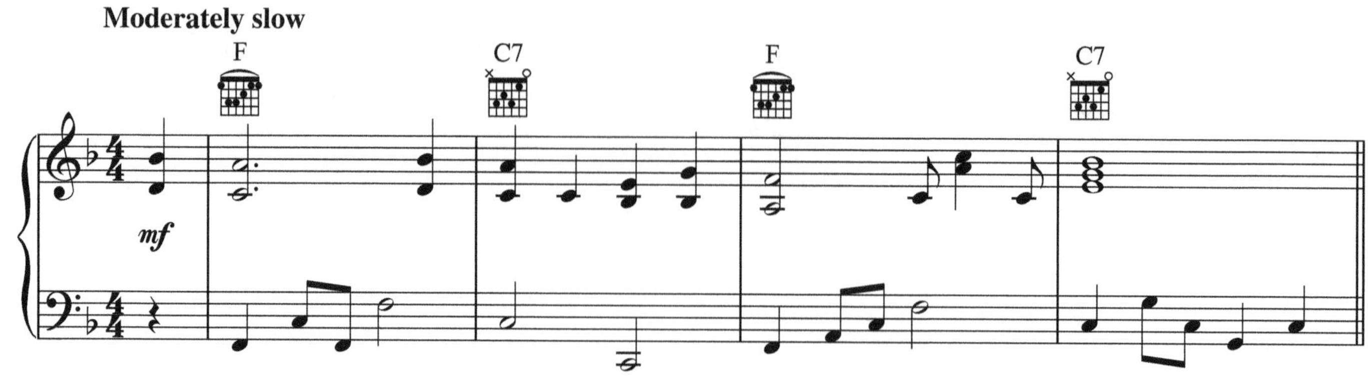

F
C7
F
Fdim
B♭6/F
F
F7
8fr
more. To waste our lives would be a
near. Her lips are warm while yours are
me? To live a lie would bring us

B♭
F
C7
sin; re - lease me and let me love a -
cold; re - lease me, my dar - ling, let me
pain, so re - lease me and let me love a -

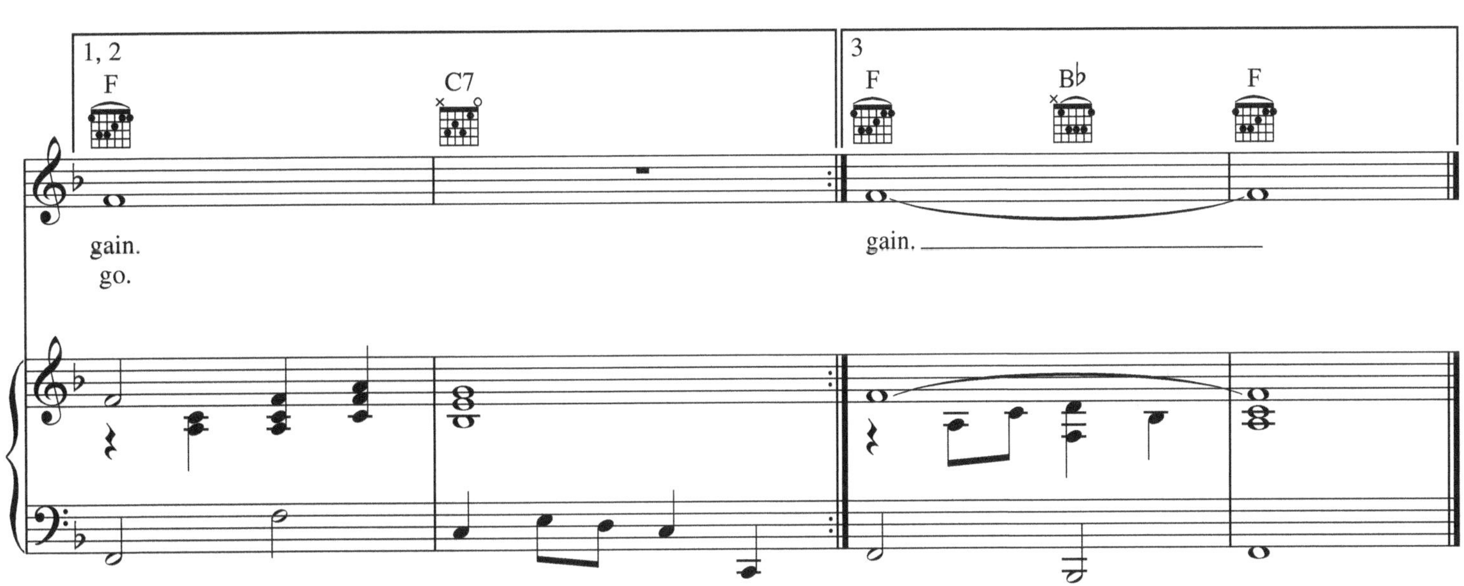
1, 2
3
F
C7
F
B♭
F
gain.
go.
gain.

RUB-A-DUB-DUB

Words and Music by
HANK THOMPSON

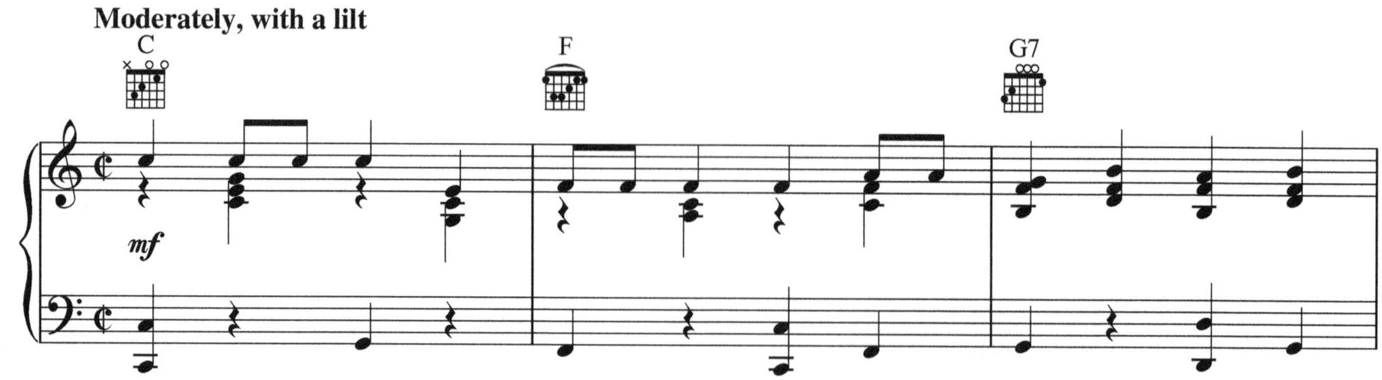

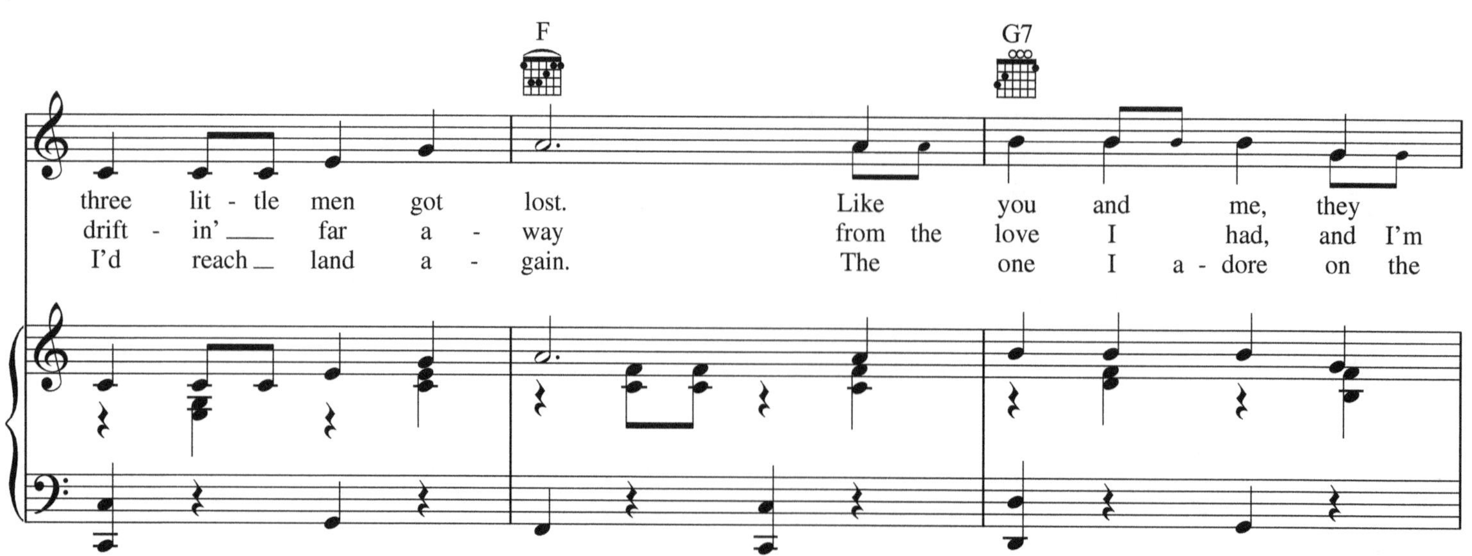

couldn't a - gree, and up - on the waves they
feel - in' might - y bad, and I can't go on this
dis - tant shore is ___ at the rain - bow's
C
tossed. I'll sing their tune 'cause I got ma - rooned with a
way. Won't you throw out the line and ___ say you're mine and ___
end. To the three lit - tle guys I ___ turned my eyes. Won't you
F
G7
love I can't for - get. Now, the three lit - tle men just
take me back a - gain? 'Cause my rud - der's broke and it
tell your names to me? Well, ___ one said, ___ "Fate," and
took me in on an o - cean of re -
ain't no joke. Won't you reach and pull me
one said, "Hate," and the oth - er said, "Jeal - ous -

C
F
G7
C
gret.
in?
y."
With a rub - a - dub - dub, three men in a tub,
G7
C
lost on the o - cean blue. I'll row like a hub, sing
F
G7
1, 2
C
F
rub - a - dub - dub, 'cause you broke my heart in two.
C
3
C
F
C
Well, I
Well, I
two.

SEND ME THE PILLOW YOU DREAM ON

Words and Music by
HANK LOCKLIN

F
C
Send me the pil - low that you dream on,
G7
so, dar - ling, I can dream on it
C
C7
F
too.
Each night while I'm
wait - ed so
C
sleep - ing, oh, so lone - ly,
long for you to write me,
I'll
but

G7
C
share your love in dreams that once were true;
just a mem - 'ry's all that's left of you;
F
send me the pil - low that you
C
G7
dream on, so dar - ling, I can dream on it
1
C
C7
too. I've
2
C
F
C/E
Dm7
C
too.

A SATISFIED MIND

Words and Music by JOE "RED" HAYES
and JACK RHODES

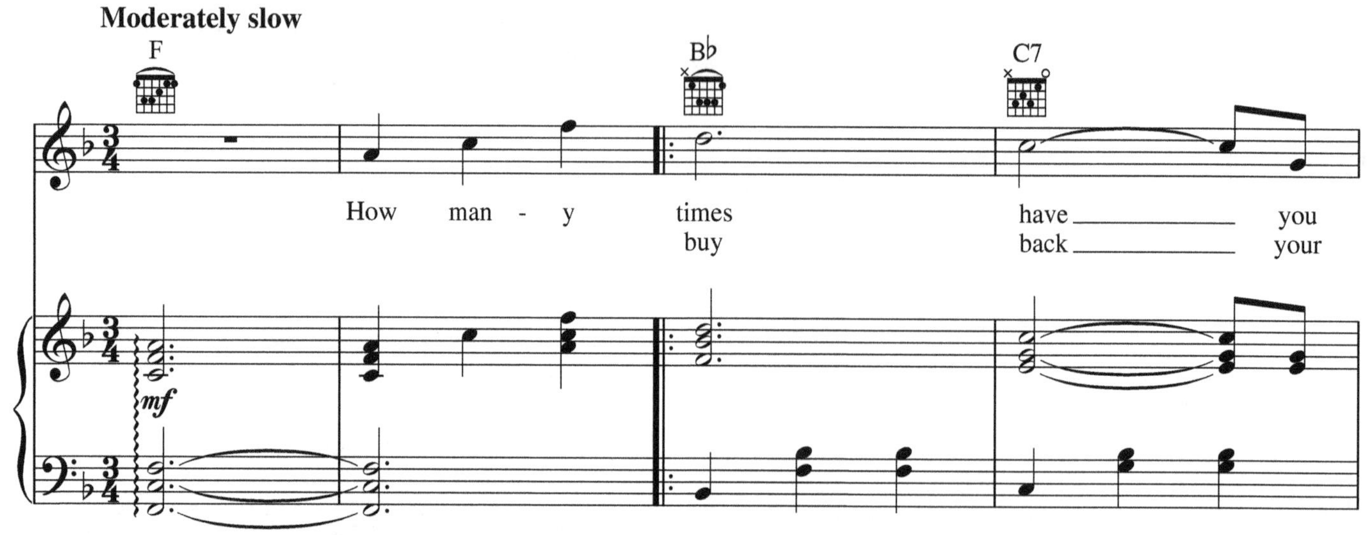

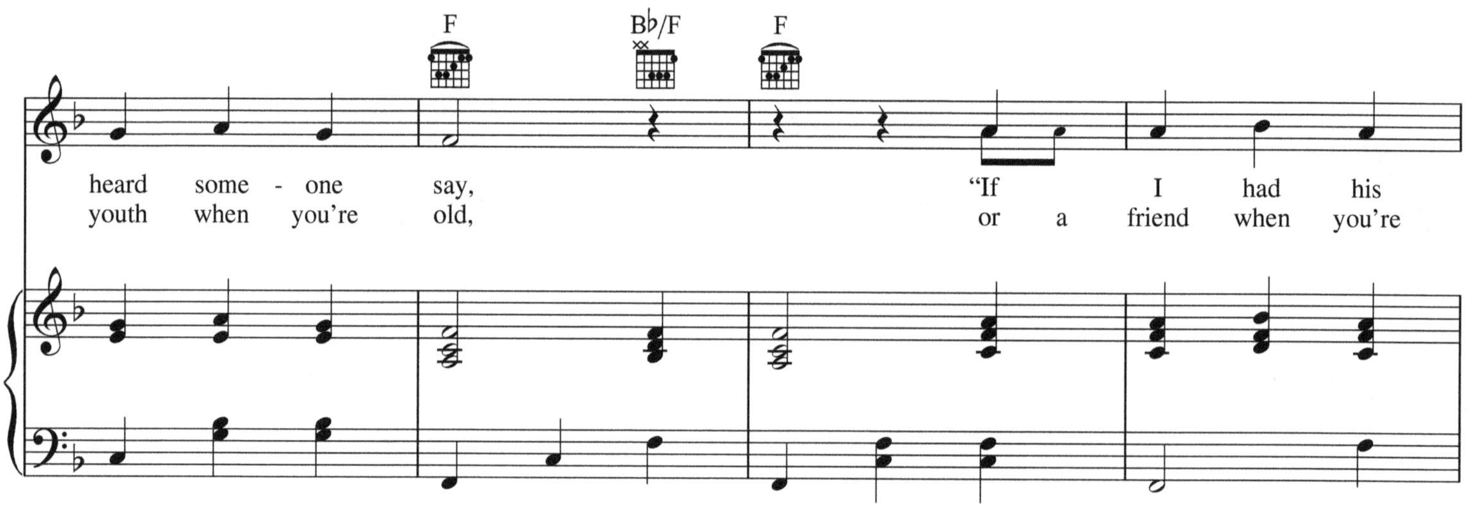

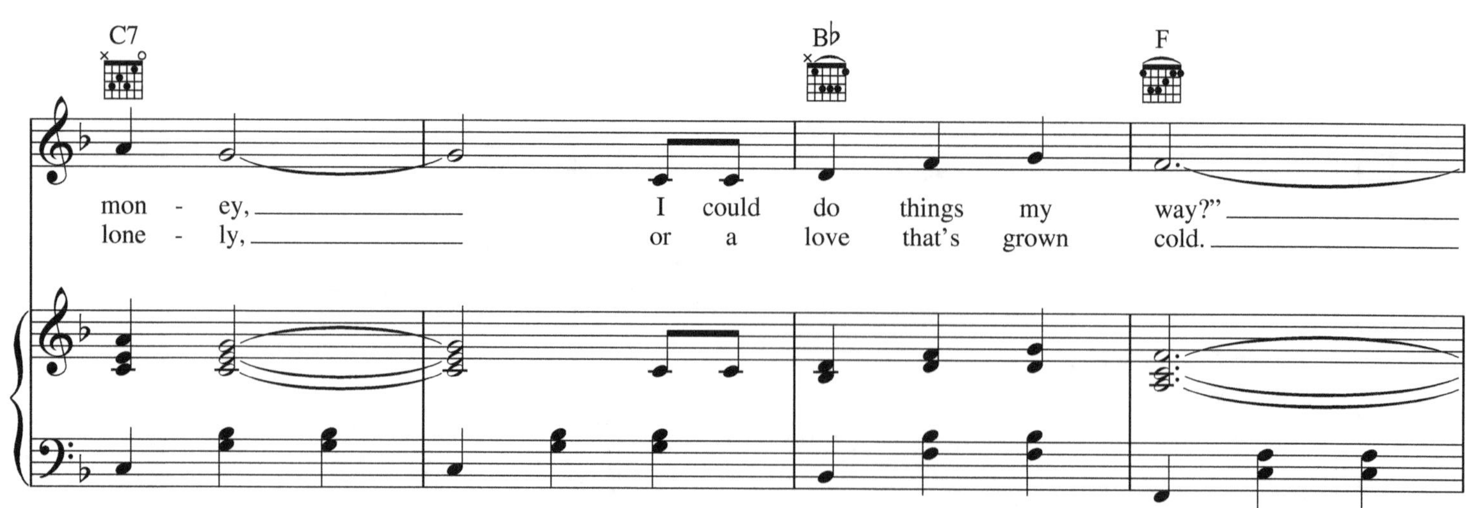

C7
But lit - tle they know that it's
The wealth - i - est per - son is a
B♭
F
so hard to find one rich man in
pau - per at times, com - pared to the
C7
B♭
F
ten with a sat - is - fied mind.
man with a sat - is - fied mind.
C7
Once I was win - ning
When life has end - ed,

B♭
F
in for - tune and fame;
my time has run out;
C7
ev - 'ry - thing that I dreamed for
my friends and my loved ones,
B♭
F
to get a start in life's game. But
I'll leave, there's no doubt. But
B♭
C7
sud - den - ly it hap - pened, I
there's one thing for cer - tain, when

F
lost ev - 'ry dime.
it comes my time.
But I'm
I'll
C7
rich - er by far
leave this old world
1
B♭
with a sat - is - fied
F
mind.
Mon - ey can't
2
B♭
F/A
Gm7
F
with a sat - is - fied mind.
molto rit. e dim.

SINGING THE BLUES

Words and Music by
MELVIN ENDSLEY

F
Bb
F
never felt more like crying all night 'cause ev-'ry-thing's wrong and
C7
Bb
C7
nothing ain't right without you. You got me singing the
F
F7
Bb
F
blues. The moon and stars no longer shine, the
Bb
F
Bb
F
dream is gone I thought was mine. There's nothing left for me to do but

C7
F
cry over you. Well, I nev-er felt more like
B♭
F
C7
run-ning a-way, but why should I go, 'cause I could-n't stay with-
B♭
C7
1
F
B♭
out you. You got me sing-ing the blues.
F
C
2
F
C7
F
Well, I blues.

SLOW POKE

Words and Music by PEE WEE KING,
CHILTON PRICE and REDD STEWART

G7
Dm7
G7
G7♯5
Cmaj7
C
C7
B7
B♭7
Time means noth - in' to you. I wait and then,
A9
5fr
Em7
A7
D7
Am7
late a - gain, eight o' - clock, nine o' - clock,
D7
Am7/D
D7
G
G♯dim7
quar - ter to ten. Why should I lin - ger ev - 'ry time you snap your fin - ger, lit - tle
Am7
D7
Am7
D7
slow - poke? Why can't you has - ten when you

Am7
D7
G
G9
9fr
G7♯5
see the time's a - wast - in'? You're a slow - poke, dear.
3
C
Am7♭5
Bm7
E9
Why should I keep try - in' to change you? It's not the thing to do. I
Am
E7
Am
D7
1
G
Em
guess I'll have to learn to be a slow - poke too!
Am7
D7♭9
4fr
2
G
Am7
G6/9
too!
3
3

SIXTEEN TONS

Words and Music by
MERLE TRAVIS

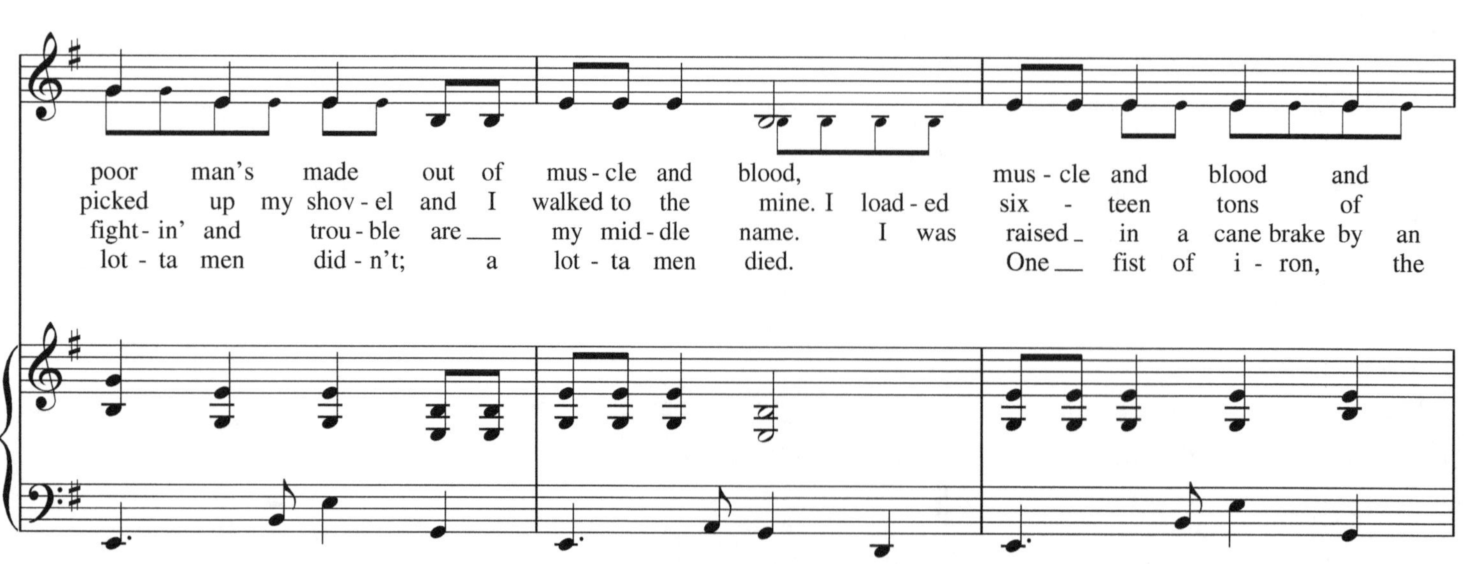

Am
C7
Em
skin and bones, a mind that's weak and a back that's strong. You load
num-ber nine coal and the straw boss said, "Well-a bless my soul." You load
ole ma-ma lion, cain't no high-toned wom-an make me walk the line. You load
oth-er of steel, if the right one don't a-get you, then the left one will. You load
six-teen tons, what do you get? An-oth-er day old-er and deep-er in debt. Saint
Am
Em
Pe-ter, don't you call me 'cause I can't go. I owe my soul to the com-pa-ny store.
1-3
B7
I was
I was
If you
4
B7
Em

SLOWLY

Words and Music by TOMMY HILL
and WEBB PIERCE

G
C
I can't hide my feel - ings, for it's so plain and
G
C
Cm
3fr
G
true. Slow - ly I'm fall - ing
Am
D7
G
A♯dim7
Am7
D7
G
more in love with you. More and more I
C
G
need you and want you by my side.

A7
More and more I love you as each day pass - es
D7
G
by. No need to hide my feel - ings, for
C
G
C
Cm
3fr
it's so plain and true. Slow - ly I'm
G
Am
D7
G
fall - ing more in love with you.

TENNESSEE WALTZ

Words and Music by REDD STEWART
and PEE WEE KING

G
G7
duced him to my loved one and while they were
C
G
D7
waltz - ing my friend stole my sweet - heart from
G
me.
I re - mem - ber the
B7
C
G
night and the Ten - nes - see Waltz.
Now I know just how

D7
much I have lost. Yes, I
G
G7
lost my lit - tle dar - lin' the night they were
C
G
D7
play - ing the beau - ti - ful Ten - nes - see
1
G
Waltz. I was
2
G
Waltz.

THE THREE BELLS

Words and Music by BERT REISFELD
and JEAN VILLARD

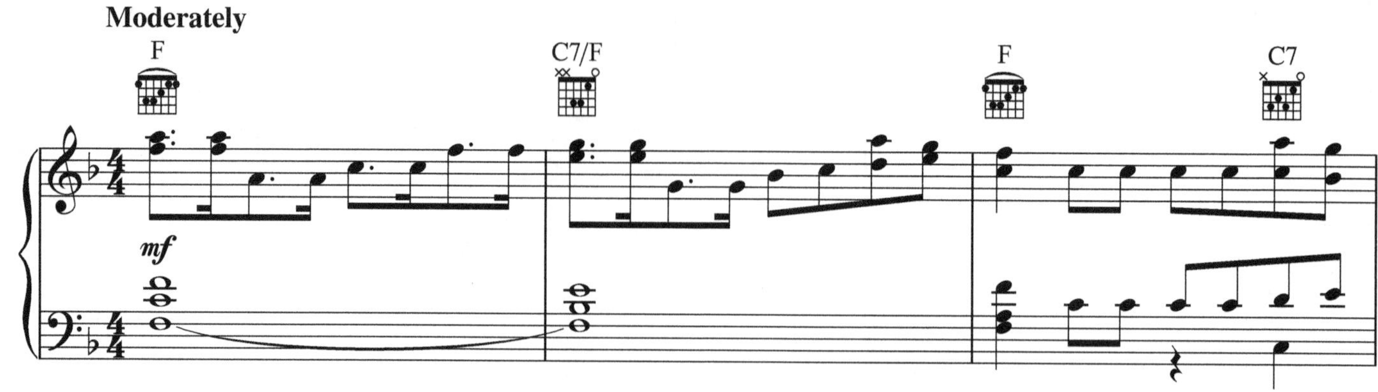

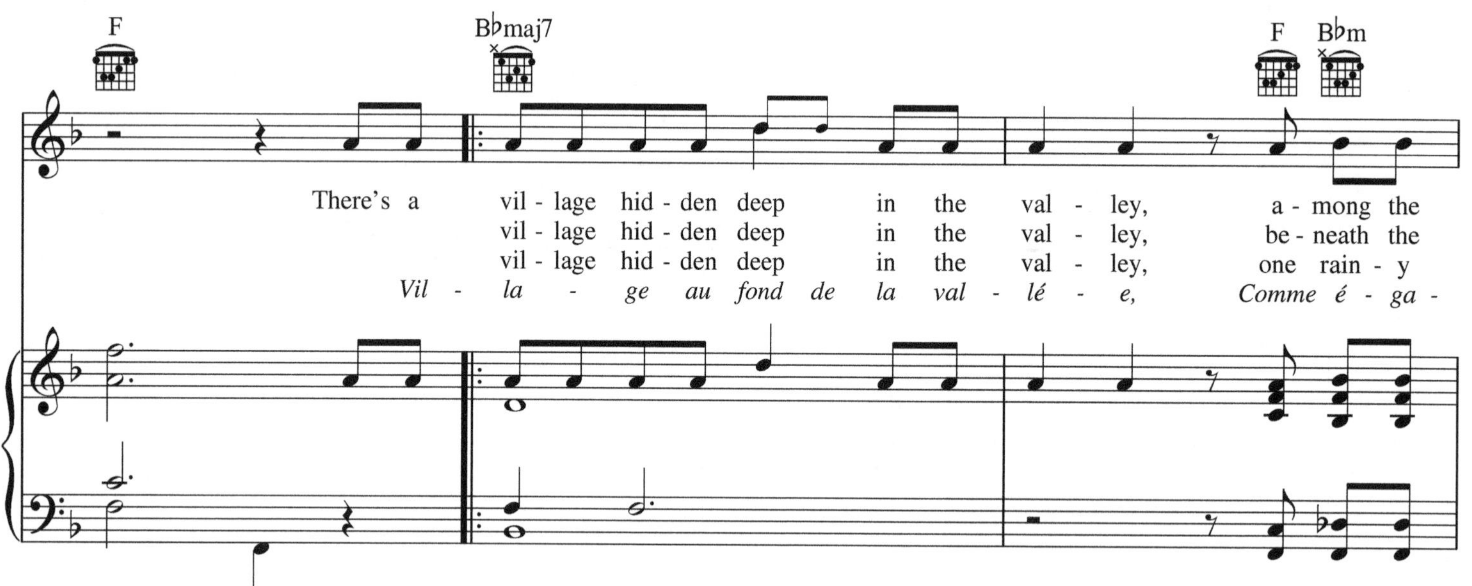

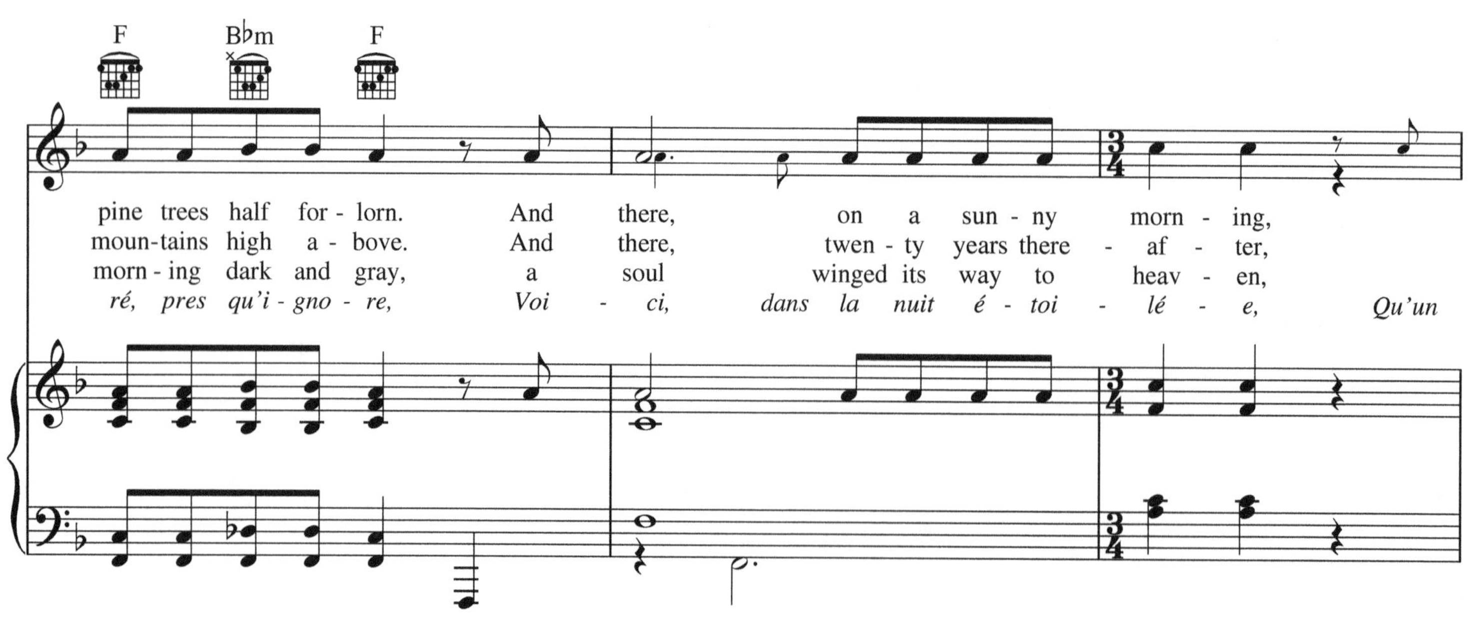

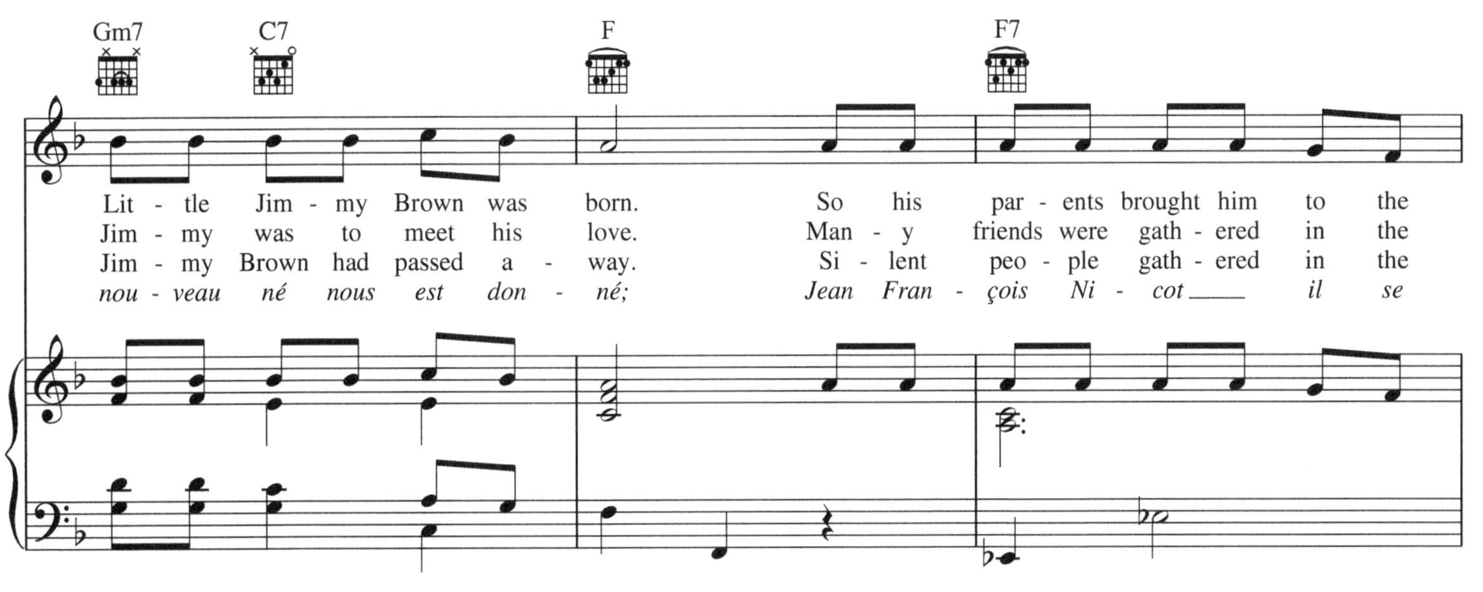
Gm7 C7 F F7
Lit - tle Jim - my Brown was born. So his par - ents brought him to the
Jim - my was to meet his love. Man - y friends were gath - ered in the
Jim - my Brown had passed a - way. Si - lent peo - ple gath - ered in the
nou - veau né nous est don - né; Jean Fran - çois Ni - cot il se

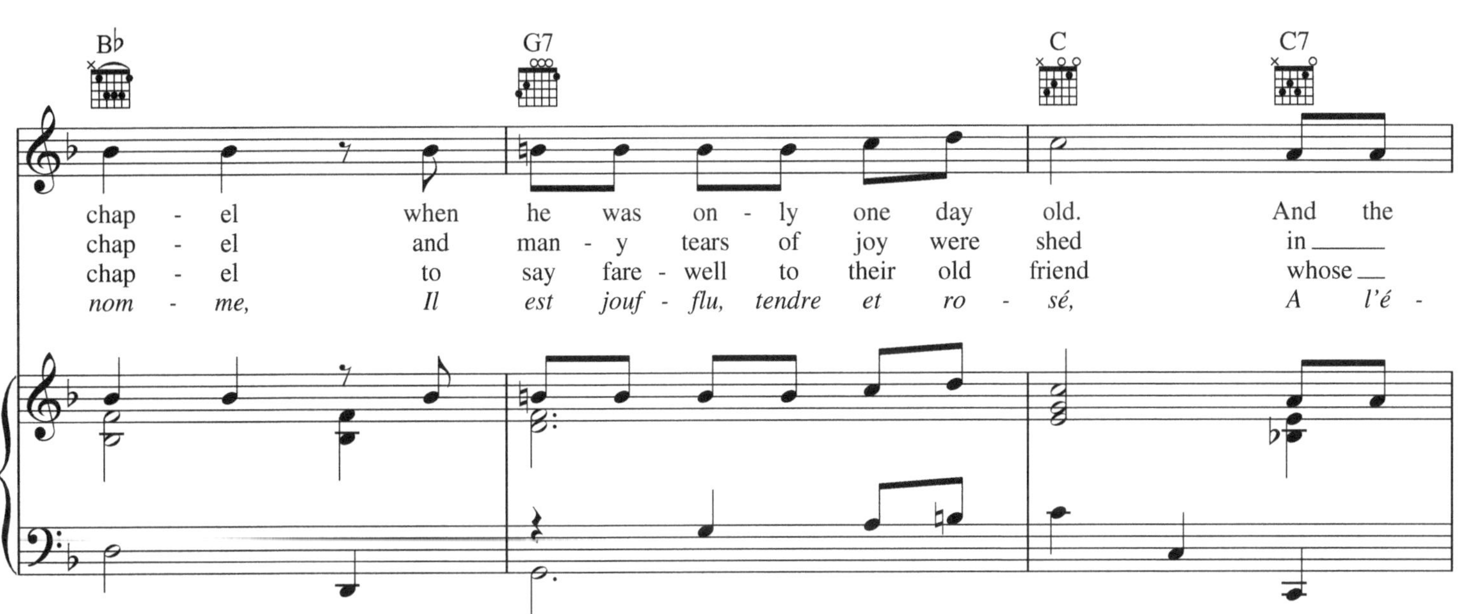
B♭ G7 C C7
chap - el when he was on - ly one day old. And the
chap - el and man - y tears of joy were shed in
chap - el to say fare - well to their old friend whose
nom - me, Il est jouf - flu, tendre et ro - sé, A l'é -

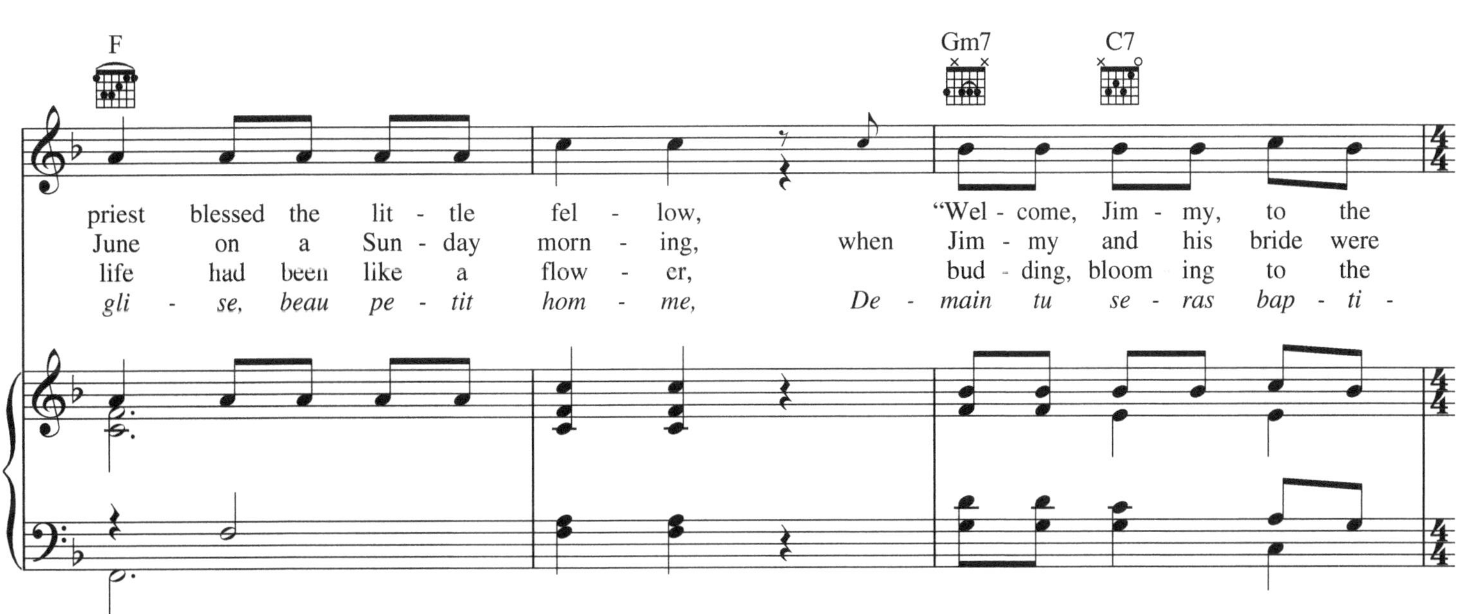
F Gm7 C7
priest blessed the lit - tle fel - low, "Wel - come, Jim - my, to the
June on a Sun - day morn - ing, when Jim - my and his bride were
life had been like a flow - er, bud - ding, bloom ing to the
gli - se, beau pe - tit hom - me, De - main tu se - ras bap - ti -

F
N.C.
fold." All the chap - el bells were
wed. All the chap - el bells were
end. Just a lone - ly bell was
sé. U - ne clo - che son - ne,

B♭
ring - ing in the lit - tle val - ley
ring - ing. 'Twas a great day in his
ring - ing in the lit - tle val - ley
son - ne, Sa voix d'é - chos en é -

F
F7
town. And the songs that they were sing - ing
life, 'cause the songs that they were sing - ing
town. 'Twas fare-well that it was sing - ing
chos, Dit au mon - de qui s'é - ton - ne:

B♭
was for ba - by Jim - my Brown.
was for Jim - my and his wife.
to our good old Jim - my Brown.
C'est pour Jean Fran - çois Ni - cot!

Then the lit - tle con - gre - ga - tion
Then the lit - tle con - gre - ga - tion
And the lit - tle con - gre - ga - tion
C'est pour accue il - lir une â - me

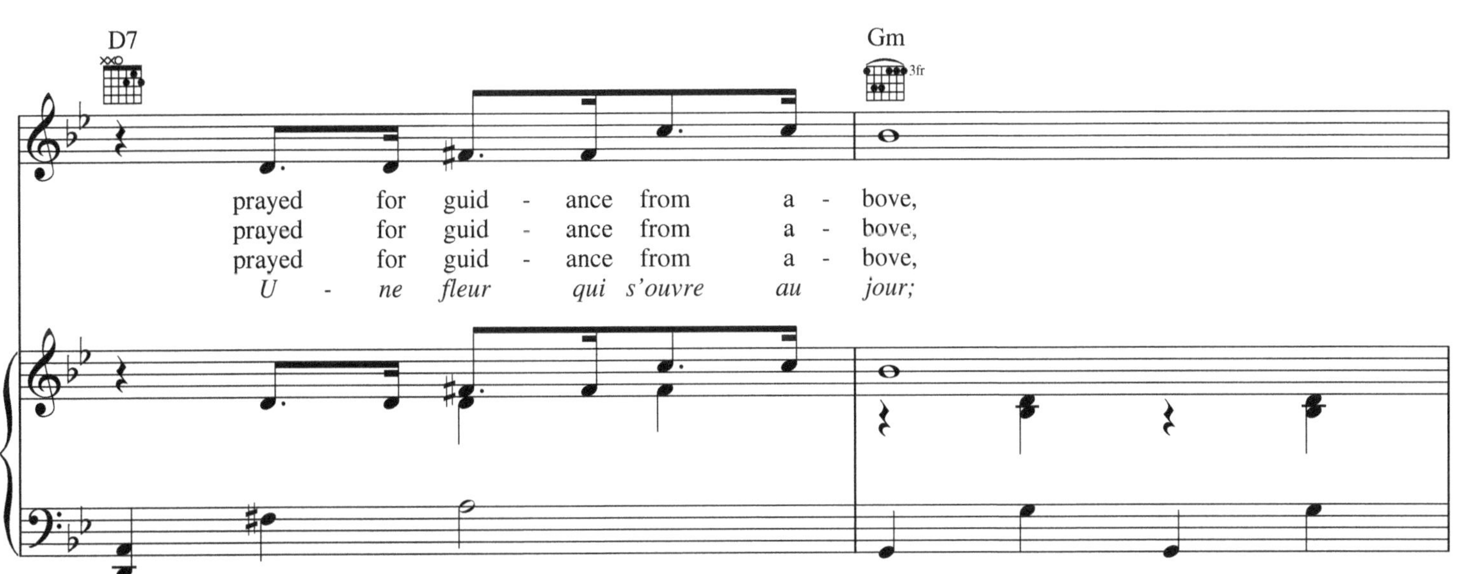
D7
Gm
3fr
prayed for guid - ance from a - bove,
prayed for guid - ance from a - bove,
prayed for guid - ance from a - bove,
U - ne fleur qui s'ouvre au jour;

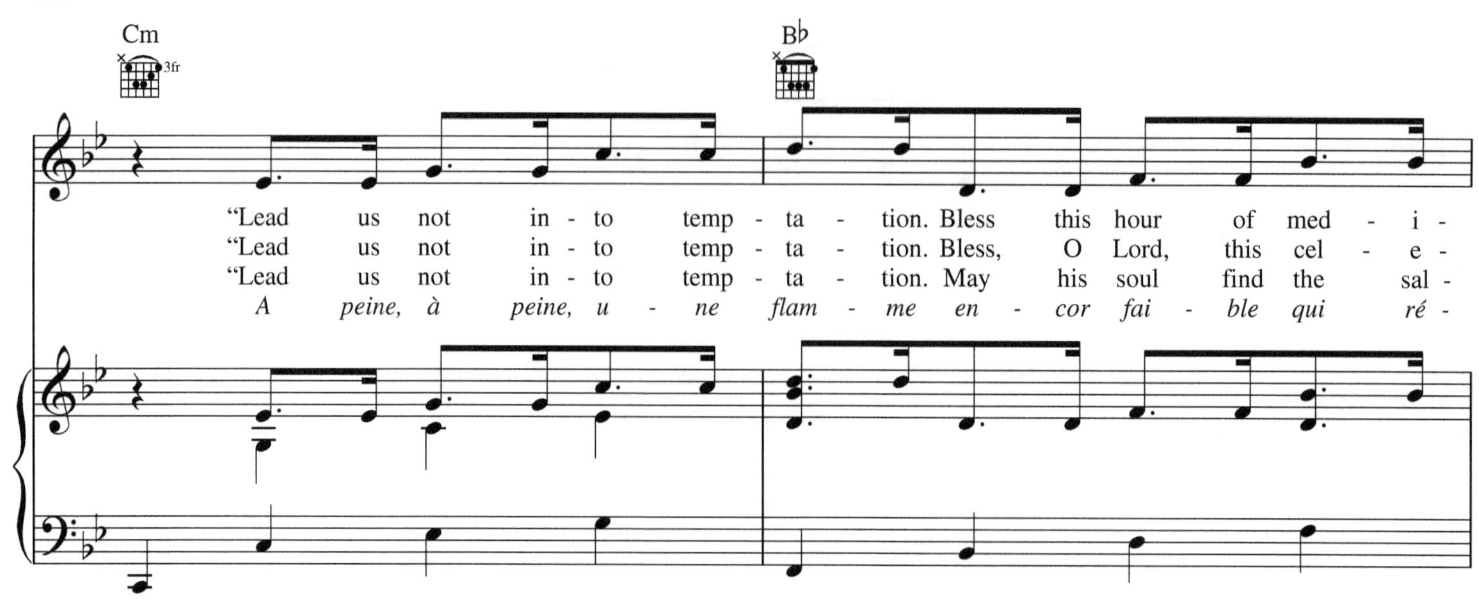
Cm
3fr
B♭
"Lead us not in - to temp - ta - tion. Bless this hour of med - i -
"Lead us not in - to temp - ta - tion. Bless, O Lord, this cel - e -
"Lead us not in - to temp - ta - tion. May his soul find the sal -
A peine, à peine, u - ne flam - me en - cor fai - ble qui ré -

F7
1, 2
B♭
ta - tion. Guide him with e - ter - nal love."
bra - tion. May their lives be filled with love."
va - tion of Thy great e - ter - nal
cla - me Pro - tec - tion ten - dresse a - mour.

F
3
B♭
F7
B♭
There's a love."
From the
Vil - mour.

WALKIN' AFTER MIDNIGHT

Lyrics by DON HECHT
Music by ALAN W. BLOCK

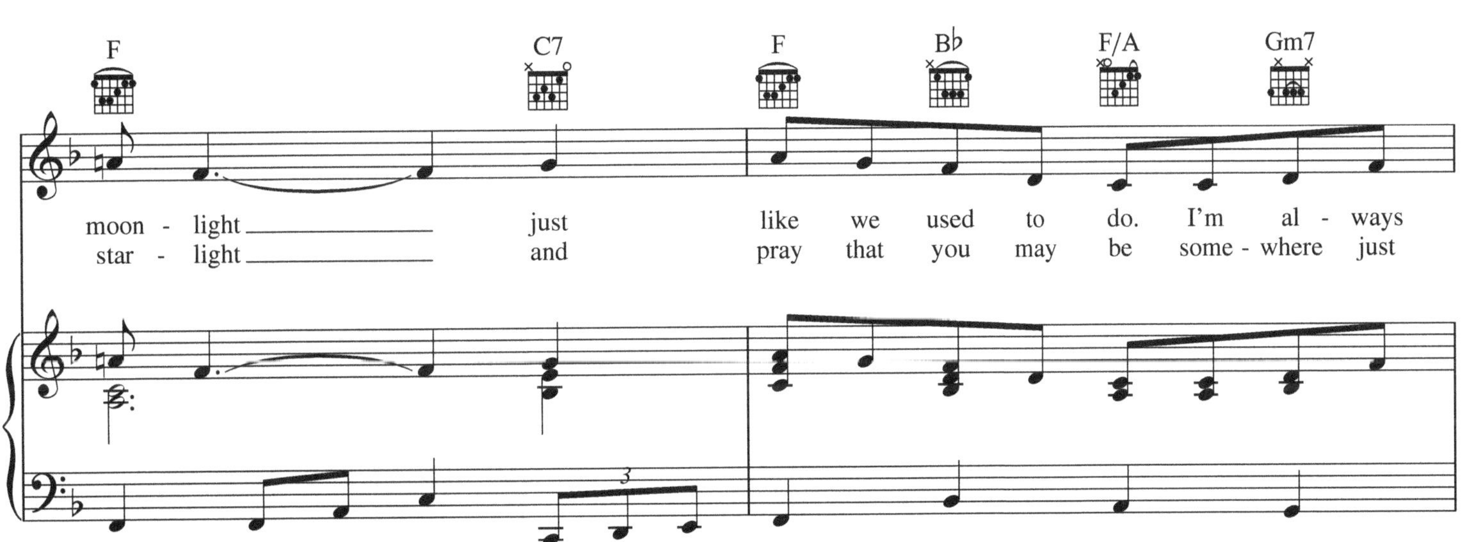

To Coda
F
B♭7
F
Gm7
walk - in' af - ter mid-night search - in' for you.
walk - in' af - ter mid-night search - in' for
F
Gm
3fr
F/A
Gm7
F
B♭7
I'll walk for miles a - long the high - way, that's just
F
C7
F
B♭
F/A
Gm7
my way of be - ing close to you. I go out
F
B♭7
F
B♭
walk - in' af - ter mid-night search - in' for you.

F
F9
Cm7
3fr
B♭
E♭7
I stop to see a weep-in' wil-low cry-in' on his pil-low,
Fmaj7
F6
F7
may-be he's cry-in' for me. And as the sky turns gloom-y,
Adim
night winds whis-per to me. I'm lone-ly as lone-ly as can
Gm7
C7
D.S. al Coda
be. I'll go out
CODA
me.
rit.

WAKE UP LITTLE SUSIE

Words and Music by BOUDLEAUX BRYANT
and FELICE BRYANT

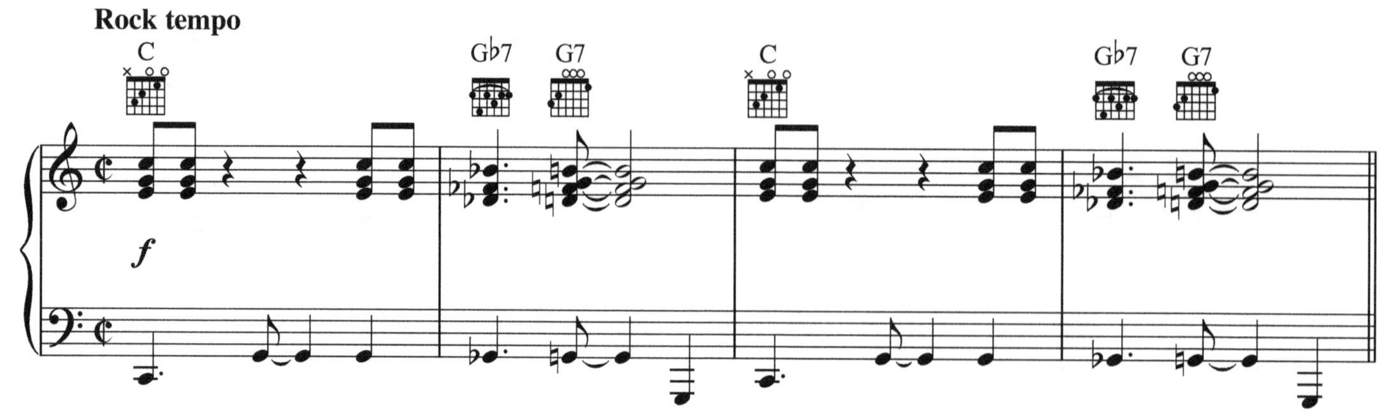

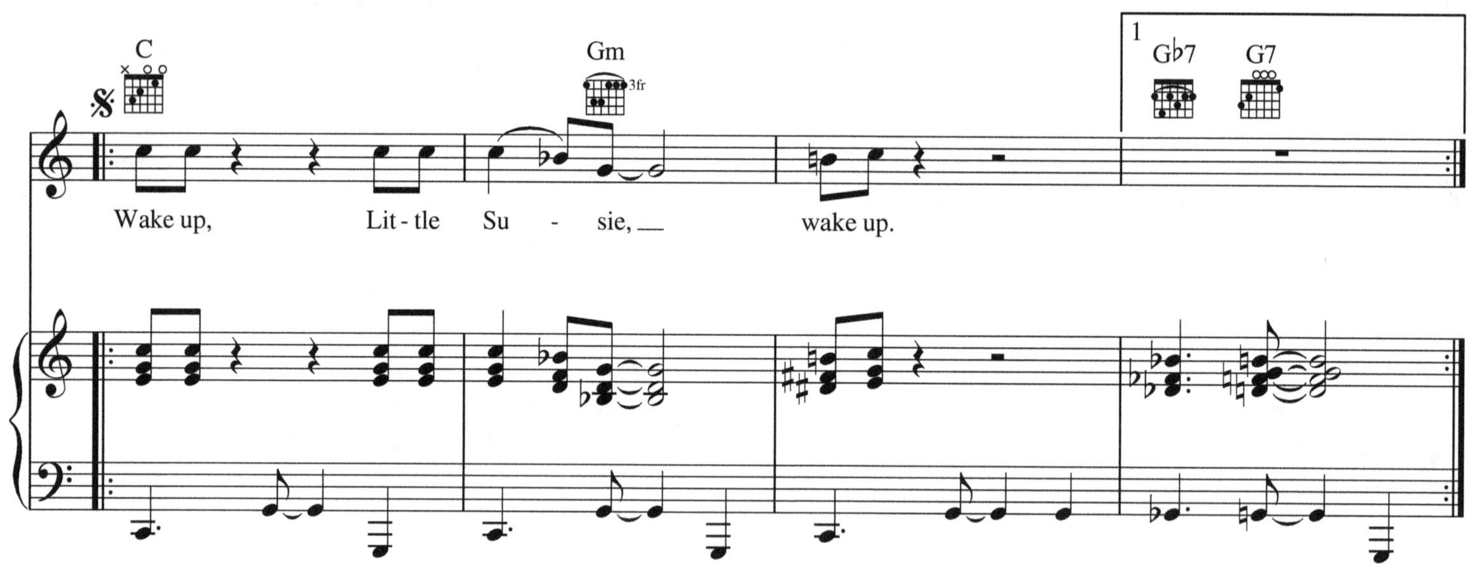

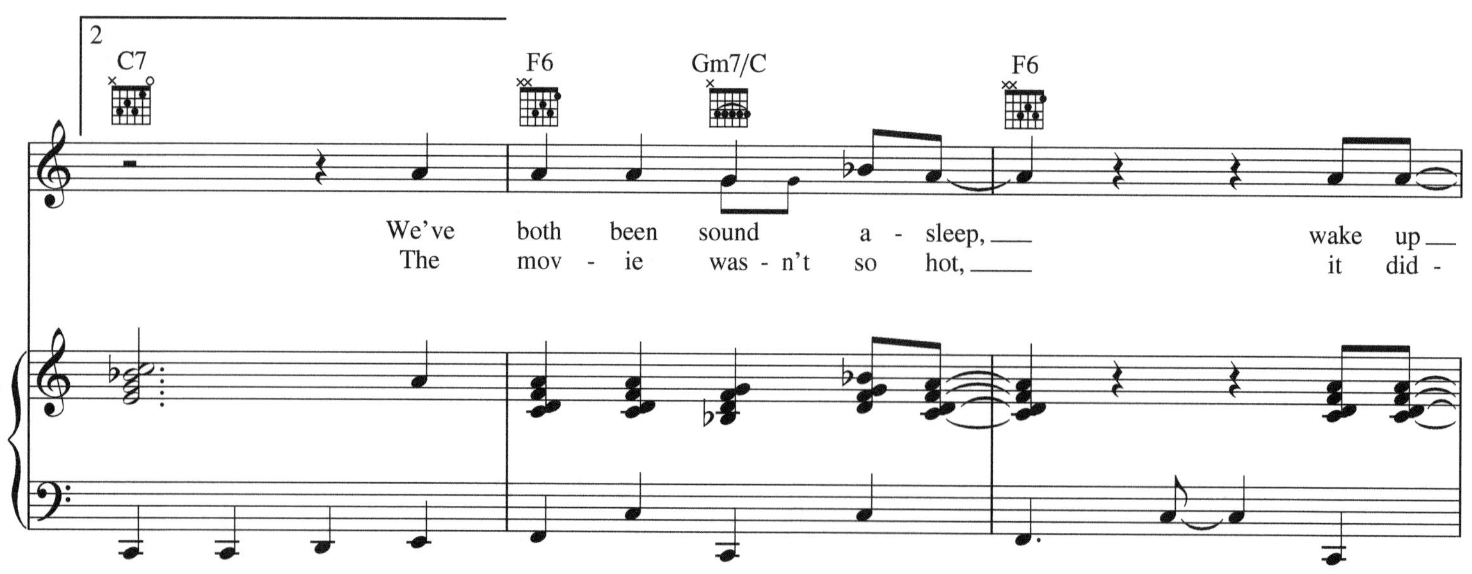

Gm7/C
F6
Gm7/C
Lit - tle Su - sie and weep. The mov - ie's o - ver, it's
- n't have much of a plot. We fell a - sleep, and our
F6
Gm7/C
F
Gm7/C
F6
four o' - clock and we're in trou - ble deep.
goose is cooked, our rep - u - ta - tion is shot.
Wake up, Lit - tle
G7
F6
G7
Su - sie. Wake up, Lit - tle Su - sie.
F7
G6
D7
G6
Well, what are we gon - na tell your ma - ma?

D7
G6
D7
What are we gon - na tell your pa?
What are we gon - na tell our friends
G
Am7
D7
G6
G7
when they say, "Ooh la la"? Wake up, Lit - tle
C6
G7
To Coda
C6
G7
Su - sie. Wake up, Lit - tle Su - sie. Well, we
C6
C7
told your ma - ma that we'd be in by ten. Well,

F6
Su - sie, ba - by, looks like we goofed a - gain.
Wake up, Lit - tle
G7
F6
G7
Su - sie.
Wake up, Lit - tle Su - sie.
We've got - ta go
C6
G♭7
D♭7
4fr
G♭7
D♭7
4fr
G♭7
G7
D.S. al Coda
(take 1st ending)
home.
CODA
C6
G♭7
G7
C6
Su - sie.

WHEN IT'S SPRINGTIME IN ALASKA
(It's Forty Below)

Words and Music by
TILLMAN B. FRANKS

C7
cit - y was a - boom. So I took a lit - tle
man's blood run cold: "When it's spring - time in A -
F Bb F Bb7 F
1
stroll to the Red Dog Sa - loon. As I
las - ka, it's for - ty be -
2
F Bb7 F
low." It was red - head - ed
Car - i - bou
I was as
C7 F
Lil who was sing - in' so sweet. I reached down and
Crawl and the Griz - zly Bear Hug, we did our
in - no - cent as I could be. I did - n't know

took the snow packs off my feet. I reached for the
dance on a Ko - di - ak rug. The song she kept
Lil was Big Ed's wife - to - be. He took out his
gal who was sing - in' the tune. We did the
sing - in' made a man's blood run cold: "When it's
knife and he gave it a throw. When it's
C7
F
B♭
Es - ki - mo Hop all a - round the sa -
spring - time in A - las - ka, it's for - ty be -
spring - time in A - las - ka, I'll be six feet be -
1, 2
F
B♭7
F
loon. With the
low."
3
F
B♭7
F
low.

WHITE LIGHTNING

Words and Music by
J.P. RICHARDSON

N.C.
sun went down, then he'd fill him a jug, and he'd pass it a - round.
way I knew as my eyes bugged out and my face turned blue.
drank it on down, and I heard him a - moan - in' as he hit the ground.
F
Might - y, might - y pleas - in', Pap - py's corn squeez - in'.
E♭
3fr
B♭
N.C.
Fshew, hic - cup,
Fshew,
Fshew, hic - cup,
ooh, white light - nin'.
B♭
E♭
3fr
Well,
Yeah,
Well,
the G - men, T - men,

B♭
Rev - e - nuers, too, search - in' for the place _ where he made his brew. They were
F
E♭
3fr
B♭
N.C.
look - in', try - in' book him, but my Pap - py kept a - cook - in'
fshew, ____
fshew, ooh, __
fshew, ____
white light - nin'.
1, 2
B♭
Well, I
Well, a
3
B♭
Repeat and Fade
Optional Ending

A WHITE SPORT COAT
(And a Pink Carnation)

Words and Music by
MARTY ROBBINS

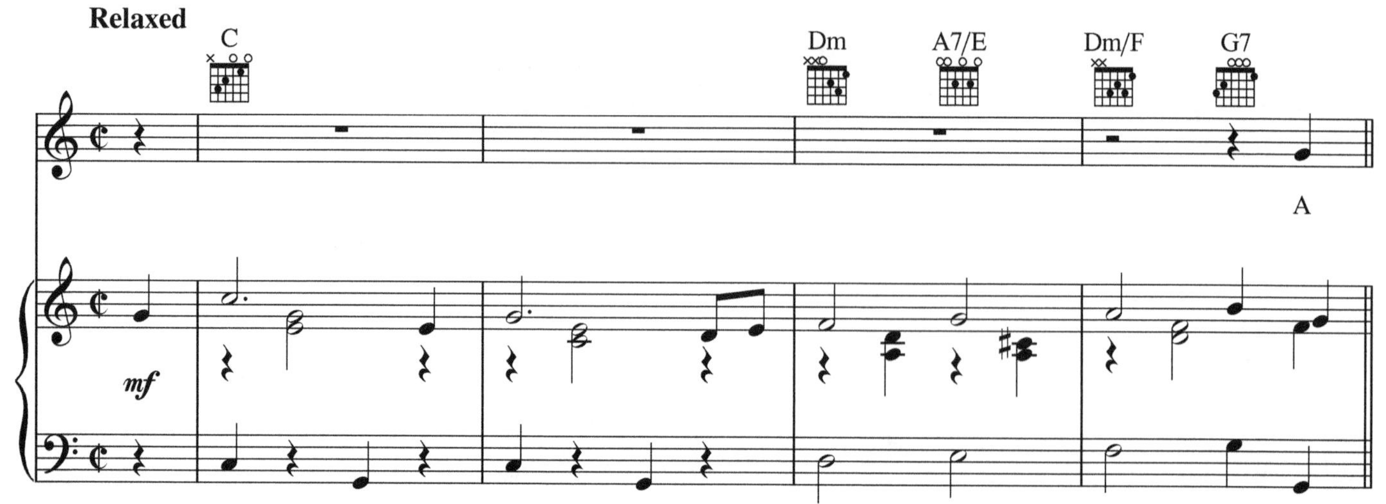

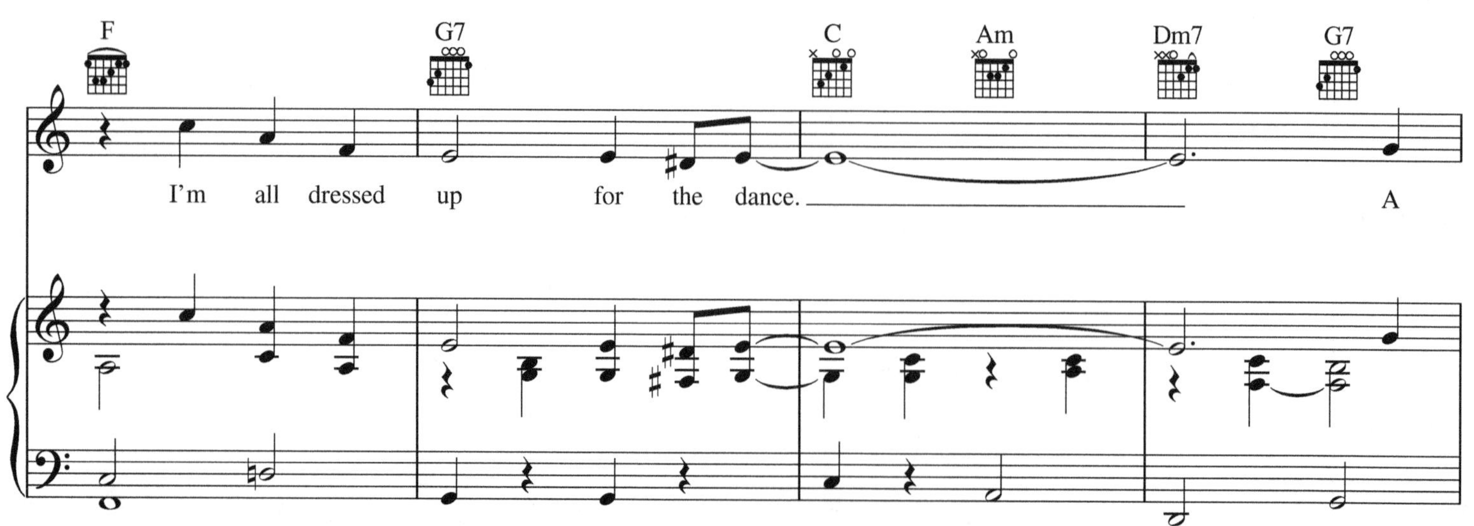

C
Dm
G7
white sport coat and a pink car - na - tion,
F
G7
C
F
C
I'm all a - lone in ro - mance.
G7
C
Once you told me long a - go
to the Prom with
D7
me you'd go.
Now you've changed your mind, it seems

G7
C
some - one else will hold my dreams. A white sport
Dm
G7
coat and a pink car - na - tion,
F
G7
1
C
C♯dim
4fr
I'm in a blue, blue mood.
Dm
G7
2
C
F
C
A mood.

YOUR CHEATIN' HEART

Words and Music by
HANK WILLIAMS

C7
F
A♭7
4fr
the whole night through. Your cheat - in'
when you'll be blue. Your cheat - in'
G7
C
heart will tell on you.
heart will tell on you.
C7
F
When tears come down like fall - in'
When tears come down like fall - in'
C
D7
rain, you'll toss a - round
rain, you'll toss a - round

G7
and call my name. You'll walk the
and call my name. You'll walk the
C
C7
F
floor the way I do.
floor the way I do.
A♭7
4fr
G7
Your cheat - in' heart will tell on
Your cheat - in' heart will tell on
1
C
G7
2
C
you. Your cheat - in' you.
rit.

YOUNG LOVE

Words and Music by
RIC CARTEY

F G7 C Am7 F G7
ev - er in my heart.
love for you or for me.
Young
C G7 F G7
love, first love, filled with true de -
C Am7 F G7 C G7 F
vo - tion. Young love, our love we share with
G7 C Am7
deep e - mo - tion.
1 F G7
2 F G7
D.S. and Fade
Young

HAL LEONARD COUNTRY DECADE SERIES

THE 1950s
50 country golden oldies, including: Ballad of a Teenage Queen • Cold, Cold Heart • El Paso • Heartaches by the Number • Heartbreak Hotel • Hey, Good Lookin' • I Walk the Line • In the Jailhouse Now • Jambalaya (On the Bayou) • Sixteen Tons • Tennessee Waltz • Walkin' After Midnight • Your Cheatin' Heart • and more.
00311283 Piano/Vocal/Guitar $15.99

THE 1970s
41 songs, including: All the Gold in California • Coal Miner's Daughter • Country Bumpkin • The Devil Went to Georgia • The Gambler • Another Somebody Done Somebody Wrong Song • If We Make It Through December • Lucille • Sleeping Single in a Double Bed • and more.
00311285 Piano/Vocal/Guitar $15.99

THE 1980s
40 country standards, including: All My Ex's Live in Texas • The Chair • Could I Have This Dance • Coward of the County • Drivin' My Life Away • Elvira • Forever and Ever, Amen • God Bless the U.S.A. • He Stopped Loving Her Today • I Was Country When Country Wasn't Cool • Islands in the Stream • On the Road Again • Tennessee Flat Top Box • To All the Girls I've Loved Before • What's Forever For • You're the Reason God Made Oklahoma • and more.
00311282 Piano/Vocal/Guitar $15.99

THE 1990s
40 songs, including: Achy Breaky Heart (Don't Tell My Heart) • Amazed • Blue • Boot Scootin' Boogie • Down at the Twist and Shout • Friends in Low Places • The Greatest Man I Never Knew • He Didn't Have to Be • Here's a Quarter (Call Someone Who Cares) • Man! I Feel like a Woman! • She Is His Only Need • Wide Open Spaces • You Had Me from Hello • You're Still the One • and more.
00311280 Piano/Vocal/Guitar $16.95

THE 2000s - 2nd Edition
35 contemporary country classics, including: Alcohol • American Soldier • Beer for My Horses • Blessed • Breathe • Have You Forgotten? • I Am a Man of Constant Sorrow • I Hope You Dance • I'm Gonna Miss Her (The Fishin' Song) • Long Black Train • No Shoes No Shirt (No Problems) • Redneck Woman • Where the Stars and Stripes and the Eagle Fly • Where Were You (When the World Stopped Turning) • and more.
00311281 Piano/Vocal/Guitar $16.99

FOR MORE INFORMATION,
SEE YOUR LOCAL MUSIC DEALER,
OR WRITE TO:

HAL•LEONARD®
CORPORATION
7777 W. BLUEMOUND RD. P.O. BOX 13819
MILWAUKEE, WISCONSIN 53213
Visit Hal Leonard online at
www.halleonard.com

Contemporary & Classic Country

More great country hits from Hal Leonard arranged for piano and voice with guitar chords.

The Best Country Songs Ever – 2nd Edition
This outstanding collection features 78 country favorites: Always on My Mind • Blue • Crying • Daddy Sang Bass • Friends in Low Places • God Bless the U.S.A. • He Stopped Loving Her Today • I Fall to Pieces • King of the Road • Love Without End, Amen • Mammas Don't Let Your Babies Grow Up to Be Cowboys • Rhinestone Cowboy • Stand by Your Man • Wabash Cannonball • more.
00359135 .... $17.95

Country Gospel U.S.A.
Piano/guitar/4-part vocal arrangements of 50 well-known country/gospel songs: An American Trilogy • Daddy Sang Bass • I Saw the Light • Love Lifted Me • Mansion over the Hilltop • Turn Your Radio On • Will the Circle Be Unbroken.
00240139 .... $10.95

Country Legends
A budget-priced collection of 50 favorites from country music's finest. Includes: Blue Eyes Crying in the Rain • Down at the Twist and Shout • Help Me Make It Through the Night • I Fought the Law • Mountain Music • Tie a Yellow Ribbon Round the Ole Oak Tree • Walkin' After Midnight • You Are My Sunshine • Your Cheatin' Heart • and more.
00315339 .... $12.95

Country Love Songs – 4th Edition
This edition features 34 romantic country favorites, including: Amazed • Breathe • For the Good Times • I Need You • The Keeper of the Stars • Love Can Build a Bridge • One Boy, One Girl • Stand by Me • This Kiss • Through the Years • Valentine • more.
00311528 .... $14.95

Country Songs – Budget Book
You get a lot of bang for your buck with this great collection of 90 songs for only $12.95! Titles include: All My Ex's Live in Texas • Boot Scootin' Boogie • Cowboy Take Me Away • Elvira • Hey, Good Lookin' • Lucille • Okie from Muskogee • Sixteen Tons • and many more!
00310833 .... $12.95

Prices, contents, and availability subject to change without notice.

Country Standards
PIANO PLAY ALONG, VOLUME 6
Practice and perform with professional-sounding accompaniments on CD to match 8 songs in the book. Includes: Blue Eyes Crying in the Rain • Crazy • King of the Road • Oh, Lonesome Me • Ring of Fire • Tennessee Waltz • You Are My Sunshine • Your Cheatin' Heart.
00311077 Book/CD Pack $12.95

Good Ol' Country
58 old-time favorites: Candy Kisses • Cold, Cold Heart • Crazy • Crying in the Chapel • Deep in the Heart of Texas • Faded Love • Green Green Grass of Home • Hey, Good Lookin' • I Can't Stop Loving You • Sweet Dreams • Tennessee Waltz • You Are My Sunshine • You Don't Know Me • more.
00310517 .... $14.95

The Grand Ole Opry Songbook
80 songs from 80 years of country music are featured in this collection: Coal Miner's Daughter (Loretta Lynn) • Green Green Grass of Home (Porter Wagoner) • I Was Country When Country Wasn't Cool (Barbara Mandrell) • When You Say Nothing at All (Alison Krauss) • and more. Includes photos and articles.
00311248 .... $19.95

COUNTRY MUSIC TELEVISION'S
100 Greatest Songs of Country Music
In 2003, Country Music Television compiled a panel of experts to rank the 100 greatest country songs of all time. This folio presents all 100 songs: Crazy (#3) • Friends in Low Places (#6) • He Stopped Loving Her Today (#2) • Ring of Fire (#4) • Stand by Your Man (#1) • Your Cheatin' Heart (#5) • and many more.
00306544 .... $29.95

COUNTRY MUSIC TELEVISION'S
100 Greatest Country Love Songs
This book provides an amazing collection of classic and contemporary country love songs as voted on by Country Music Television, including: Always on My Mind • Behind Closed Doors • Could I Have This Dance • Forever and Ever, Amen • I Fall to Pieces • Lady • Ring of Fire • Stand by Your Man • You're Still the One • and more.
00311159 .... $24.95

100 Most Wanted
Highlights: A Boy Named Sue • Break It to Me Gently • Crying My Heart out over You • Heartbroke • I.O.U. • I Know a Heartache When I See One • Mammas Don't Let Your Babies Grow Up to Be Cowboys • My Heroes Have Always Been Cowboys • Stand by Me • Save the Last Dance for Me • You're the First Time I've Thought About Leaving • You're the Reason God Made Oklahoma • many more.
00360730 .... $15.95

Top Country Hits of '04-'05
20 of the year's best from country's hottest stars: American Soldier • Back When • Days Go By • How Am I Doin' • In a Real Love • Long Black Train • Mr. Mom • Mud on the Tires • Nothin 'Bout Love Makes Sense • Party for Two • Redneck Woman • Stays in Mexico • This One's for the Girls • The Woman with You • more.
00311212 .... $14.95

20th Century Country Music
Over 70 country classics representative of a century's worth of music, including: All the Gold in California • Always on My Mind • Amazed • Blue Moon of Kentucky • Boot Scootin' Boogie • Breathe • Crazy • Friends in Low Places • Harper Valley P.T.A. • Hey, Good Lookin' • Ring of Fire • and more.
00310673 .... $19.95

Wedding Songs Country Style – 2nd Edition
An excellent selection of 35 popular "country style" wedding and love songs. New, old and unique songs are featured. Includes: The Keeper of the Stars • Marry Me • Grow Old with Me • One Boy, One Girl • Vows Go Unbroken • When You Say Nothing at All • and many others.
00310183 .... $14.95

FOR MORE INFORMATION, SEE YOUR LOCAL MUSIC DEALER, OR WRITE TO:

7777 W. BLUEMOUND RD. P.O. BOX 13819 MILWAUKEE, WI 53213

Visit Hal Leonard online at **www.halleonard.com**